"Why didn't you ever kiss me, Josh?"

Her words came out like a whisper, caressing his skin as he hovered over her.

"I always wanted you to."

Desire coursed through him at the sound of her admission.

"I haven't been kissed in years."

Her voice held a sensual quality, washing over him, weakening his resolve.

"I *need* to be kissed."

Her small hand reached up, cupped the side of his face. He found himself leaning into it even as her hand moved up and around his neck. He closed his eyes as her fingers combed through his hair, not realizing until it was too late that she was pulling him closer.

Her soft, tentative lips moved against his, leaving him powerless. He responded to her kiss, and the tiny thread on which his control was hanging snapped in an instant.

Dear Reader

This story began fifteen years ago, long before I was aware of just how it could be used. I was a young teenager, experiencing first love, when my boyfriend was tragically killed in an accident. What followed was nothing short of heartbreak and pain, before I was eventually able to see that life went on regardless.

It was in 2013 that I finally realised my healing process had come to an end. In that moment, on what would have been his thirty-third birthday, I began to ask myself the question every writer asks: *What if...?* I wondered what life would have been like if only he hadn't died that day. And so this novel was born.

It is not a biography by any means, but the story of two characters on a journey of grief and healing similar to my own. It was cathartic, writing Micah and Josh's story. You can watch them grow together as they struggle with the pain of their past and manoeuvre their way through unknown territory and burgeoning new emotions.

Even when I felt it shouldn't, life went on—the world kept spinning. It wasn't the pain that defined me, but rather the way I handled it.

I have been writing for many years, but lacked the confidence to pursue my dreams. My first step after finishing my manuscript was to get it out there. Such was my motivation for entering *So You Think You Can Write*. You can imagine my surprise when I found out that the story so near and dear to my heart had won the public's vote, awarding me a publishing contract.

I hope you enjoy reading this as much as I enjoyed writing it. And that you walk away inspired and encouraged by Micah's story.

Tanya

IF ONLY...

BY
TANYA WRIGHT

MILLS & BOON

First published in Great Britain 2014
by Mills & Boon, an imprint of Harlequin (UK) Limited,
Eton House, 18-24 Paradise Road, Richmond, Surrey, TW9 1SR

© 2014 Tanya Wright

ISBN: 978 0 263 24260 7

Harlequin (UK) Limited's policy is to use papers that are natural,
renewable and recyclable products and made from wood grown in
sustainable forests. The logging and manufacturing processes conform
to the

Tanya Wright knew from an early age that she wanted to write, but it wasn't until this year that she decided to take it more seriously. In January she completed her first manuscript, and in March IF ONLY…, her second, was born. This year marks the fifteenth anniversary of the death of her own real-life Drew. That experience is what inspired her and gave her the courage and drive to write this story.

She wants to write real stories for real people who experience real struggles, and to offer them an escape from the mundane and a little bit of hope and a happily-ever-after.

Tanya is originally from Florida, but after completing her college degree in Boston she decided to stay. She's close to her family, and their antics are what inspire many traits in her characters. She is in a constant state of creativity: writing, cake-decorating, painting and sewing. She loves serving in her church, where she sings in the worship band.

**This is Tanya Wright's first book for Modern Tempted™
and is also available in eBook format
from www.millsandboon.co.uk**

To the women in my life…

Mom, my #1 fan. Your strength and perseverance
saw me through the toughest moments.

To my sisters, Jess and Shay. Outside of the moments
of uncontrollable laughter and borderline insanity that
provide me with excellent material you are my best
friends and I could not have done any of this without you.

To my grandma for instilling in me the importance of
dreaming big and going after those dreams.

To the heroes in my life—the men who set the bar high…

Dad, my anchor; my brothers, Aaron and Brandon,
and Kade, my beautiful and amazing nephew.

And to my cousin Mark and my friend Chet for your help,
regardless of time of day or the question's stupidity.

CHAPTER ONE

WASN'T FIRE SUPPOSED to be fierce, unpredictable or even dangerous? Micah twirled a strand of her flame-colored hair, wondering how she had lost the spark associated with its vibrant strands. Had the flame been extinguished years ago, or had it been a slow, gradual fade?

She wasn't even sure anymore. It was as if the last ten years had all been a lie. She had gone through the motions of healing, of moving on, only fooling herself into believing she was past it. But this semblance of a life was all a facade. It was obvious to her now. She had only buried the pain, denied its existence.

Until now.

Half a day spent lying in her bed had done nothing to comfort her like it should. She held the teddy bear Drew had given her close to her body, trying to capture any of its comforting magic, but sadly that too was failing to comfort her. On this dreary day in October, it seemed nothing could assuage the pain. It was like a fresh wound all over again.

Her phone signaled an incoming text message. Josh's name appeared on the screen.

Just wanted to check in on you. Make sure you're doing ok. Text me back <3

She ignored it, just as she had ignored all the others she had received today. She didn't want to talk to him yet. As her closest friend, Josh had been her distraction, the one who pulled her from depression and back to the land of the living. She knew he would try to shake her from her reverie and she didn't want that. Instead she chose to stay lost in her memories for just a little longer.

Throwing her phone aside, Micah decided this pity party needed to be taken up a notch. She rolled out of bed, slipped into a pair of obnoxious but oh-so-comfortable slippers and made her way to the kitchen. Catching a glimpse of herself in the mirror on the way, she stopped to take note of her once flawless, porcelain skin, now a ghostly shade of white. She looked hollow and empty. Dark circles surrounded her sad eyes. She was in a pathetic state. The last two months of depression had taken a toll on her. Her recent weight gain and carelessness with her appearance did not help the picture before her, but it was an accurate reflection of what she felt on the inside.

Continuing to the kitchen, she headed straight to the freezer, where a pint of her favorite ice cream was stashed behind bags of frozen vegetables. She had known in advance the ice cream would be needed. Sabina, her roommate, was out running errands and would be gone for a little while longer—just enough time to start a crime-drama marathon while enjoying her frozen vice without judgment.

But based on the disapproving look on Sabina's face two hours later, judgment was what she received.

"What's going on?" Sabina's eyes took in everything, her finger hooking the rim of the empty carton of ice cream, lifting it for further examination. "Please tell me you didn't eat this entire thing by yourself. And what's with the pajamas? Did you just get out of bed?"

Micah searched her mind for something to say to defend herself against the barrage of accusations, but she had nothing. She was guilty of all the above.

"You've got to snap out of it, Micah. I know you're hurting right now. But this has got to end, and preferably soon."

"Well, it won't be today. How can I not think about him on a day like this?"

"There's a difference, though. The rest of us are celebrating his life, while you...while you've been acting like he just died. It's been ten years." Sabina threw her hand up in exasperation. "Come on. We don't have time to debate this now. You're in desperate need of a shower and we're supposed to meet everyone in two hours."

The bright city lights, wailing sirens, honking horns, aggressive drivers fighting through traffic, the slight fish smell left over from market—things that others might complain about. But for Micah it all signified one thing—Boston, her home. She loved every single bit of it: every angry Irishman, Italian mobster, historical landmark and, not to be forgotten, blessed *lobstah.*

Micah and her four friends—Josh, Sabina, Hanna and Jamie—walked the streets of Boston as if they owned the city. Of course, Sabina, a model, probably thought she did. And Hanna probably could in a few years, at the rate she was going. Micah was definitely the odd one out in this successful, good-looking group, but she had put her best foot forward tonight in a worthy attempt to fit in with them.

It was a Friday night and the city was alive despite the dropping temperatures. As they crossed the busy street together, sounds of Boston's nightlife came out to greet them. Already-drunk college students littered the streets.

One girl in particular stood out as she yelled at every passing taxi, "Do you have a breath mint? Does anyone have a freakin' breath mint?" What the heck? People were just downright crazy!

This wasn't Micah's scene, but it was a sacred night, hence the heels, fancy top and false eyelashes she'd been talked into wearing. It was probably the first time she had dressed up since last October. Her feet were already killing her in these shoes. Sabina always had a way of talking her into something she knew she would regret later.

When going out in public with someone as beautiful as her roommate, you had two choices. You could dress up, join her and pray you didn't stick out like a sore thumb, or give up entirely and throw on the yoga pants that had never actually been to a yoga class. Three hundred and sixty-four days of the year Micah chose to give up before she started and donned the yoga pants.

"Gawd, I love this city at night! Why don't we do this anymore?" Sabina twirled as she walked, arms wide open, head thrown back. She stumbled a little in her four-inch heels on the uneven cobblestone, but Jamie was quick to catch her.

"Because we have jobs and lives and because only college students and creepy old people hit up this part of Boston on a Friday night."

"If you are going to have any hope of fun tonight, you're going to have to change that attitude of yours," Hanna said as she pursed her lips and quirked her eyebrows.

"My attitude? I don't have an at—" Okay, maybe she did. "It doesn't matter, anyway. I don't plan on having any fun tonight. So there." What was she? Five?

"It's Drew's night. Fun is a requirement."

"I never agreed to that rule." She looked over at Jamie.

Although he was Drew's cousin, they had been more like brothers. She knew out of everyone that he would understand. But in his typical quiet-guy fashion, he shrugged his shoulders, telling her she was on her own.

"C'mon, Micah. Drew lived for stuff like this, so if we're really going to honor his memory like we have for years, then we need to have fun. You included. This is what he would have wanted and you know it."

"He would *not* want a droopy-faced, depressed version of his Micah," Josh said as he put his arm around her to soften his words. "I know these anniversaries are hard on you, but you've made it through nine already. What's so different about this one? You can do it. I know you can."

Micah couldn't refute that. She had done just fine these last ten years. So why was this one so hard on her?

The crisp Boston air sent a chill through her body. She pulled her coat up higher around her neck and buried in closer to Josh, allowing his sheer size to block the cold October winds whipping between the buildings.

"Cold?" Josh asked as he pulled her closer and moved his hand up and down her arm in an effort to warm her. "You care to explain why you ignored all my texts today?"

"Not really."

"So you don't deny it?"

"No. I was ignoring you."

"How much ice cream did you eat today?"

"None of your business."

"What am I going to do with you?" He kept his arm around her and flashed her one of his smiles.

"I may need to rethink my vice, though. I think I've put on five pounds in the last couple months. Even my stretchy pants are starting to feel snug."

"Now that's just bad."

"Shut up. It's a sensitive subject."

Josh's deep laughter rumbled through his chest, but he got the hint and stopped talking about it.

Every sixth of October the five of them went to the same pub in downtown Boston. They would toast to the memory of Drew and talk about favorite memories, but Micah sensed this year would be different. She couldn't quite figure out what had changed until they sat down around their usual table and ordered a round of drinks. Scanning the faces of her closest friends, she knew then that Sabina had been right. They had moved on while she was still stuck—stuck in her painful memories.

The truth hit her like a ton of bricks. She had been living in denial. It was a comfortable and easy place to live. Never addressing reality. Never addressing the pain. Never allowing herself to truly grieve the loss of her first love—her only love.

Jamie raised his glass. "Here's to Drew."

Five glasses lifted in unison as she wondered if they all knew what she had just come to realize. Did they know she hadn't dealt with her grief? Were they okay with that? She continued to watch them. It was if they were all thinking the same thing: *What now?*

The guys turned their attention to the game playing on the TVs around them. The girls were playing with their phones. For a moment Micah wondered if this might be the last of the tradition she held so sacred.

Hanna's phone buzzed. "I've got to take this. I'll be right back."

Sabina had been whisked away by a group of guys, while Josh had seen some friends at the bar, leaving Jamie and Micah alone. Silence stretched between them. Running her finger across the top of her glass, she wasn't sure what to say. Her mind was still trying to grasp its latest discovery.

Her mother had taken her to a counselor when the tragedy first happened. The counselor hadn't said much, just listened while Micah talked through the emotions that were affecting every area of her life. She'd walked away from the session deciding she wouldn't let the pain control her anymore.

Micah had been certain that her grief could be controlled and normalcy restored. So every year, she allowed herself a period of time to grieve. There was no point in thinking about it or dwelling on it all the time. By limiting herself she was able to ignore the pain until eventually she became numb to it. That was how she had survived.

But as the ten-year anniversary approached, she'd sensed this one would be a more difficult to get through, and allowed herself some extra time. However, she'd failed to anticipate the extent of just how difficult it would be. Thoughts of what her life could have been, what she and Drew might have been doing now.

Micah caught Jamie looking down at his watch. "You have somewhere to be?"

"Actually, yeah. I've got a ton of work to do back at the house." He dragged his hand down his face. He looked physically and emotionally drained.

"On a Friday night?"

"Yeah. On a farm, my job is never ending. Sorry to do this to you, but I really should go."

"Fine. Go."

He pressed a quick kiss on her cheek and headed out. Micah shook her head. Jamie was the last one she'd expected to cut out on this ritual. If Jamie could give up on

it so easily, then maybe this faithful five wasn't as indestructible as she had once thought.

The fact that he had bailed on this commitment, this
promise they had made, poured anger into her cocktail
of raging emotions. Sure, by now they should all have
moved on. But show some respect. This was a tradition
among friends. Sacred. It was honoring the memory of a
friend they all held dear. But now they acted as if Drew
didn't matter to them anymore. Was she the only one
who felt this cavernous hole where he'd once existed?

Of course, she had been oblivious to it until recently.
Numb to the pain that had festered over time. And just
when she had let it out, it was like a snowball, building
and building until her grief was out of control. She took
a deep swallow of her drink and finished it off, then
reached for the ones Hanna and Sabina had left behind.

Years ago, her sadness had seemed like something
she could handle with a modicum of ease. So where had
she gone wrong? Somewhere along the way, her desire to
control the pain had stifled her grieving process. Things
that should have been dealt with years ago had been left
unaddressed.

Everything was out of hand. She had lost control. Control of her grief, her emotions, *her life.*

Enough was enough. It had been ten years. Tomorrow it would end. She would make it. Maybe finally addressing the denial and the postponed grief was a good
thing. She needed to clear it from her system. She would
allow herself one more night of sadness, top it off with
a lot of drinking, and tomorrow she would put a stop to
this once and for all. No more. Tomorrow she would take
her life back.

Her eyes scanned the pub for her other friends. Sabina
and Josh were the group's token flirts. They had capti-

vated the room, their good looks and irresistible charm creating quite a stir. Sabina's exotic beauty demanded attention everywhere they went.

Josh didn't have to move. He stood next to the bar and the women flocked all around him like vultures sinking their claws into their prey. Little did they know, Josh was far from being prey. *Beware, ladies. Beware.*

When the waitress brought the appetizers to the table, Micah ordered another drink. People always said you could drown your sorrows in alcohol, and tonight seemed like a good enough time to try.

Josh came back over to the table. "Where did everyone go?"

"Hanna had to take a call. Sabina is over there, and Jamie left."

"He left?" Josh appeared to be just as upset as she was.

"Yup."

"Real cool." Josh seemed to study her. He had a way of doing that. He could have her figured out in minutes and she hated it. "What's with you?"

She shrugged her shoulders. There just wasn't an easy answer. She had a tendency to bottle up her emotions, and tonight it seemed as though the bottle was full and running over.

She envied her friends. They seemed to have their acts together, and were experiencing so much more in life than she was. She hadn't seen it until now. Everything in her life was safe—her job, her friends. She steered away from new friendships, new relationships, new opportunities. Outside of her comfort zone she was susceptible, vulnerable. Her friends had been experiencing life while she was safe in her comfortable cocoon, far from things that could hurt her.

Now all that she had overlooked or failed to deal with

had come back to haunt her. She wanted to feel alive again, not the life of denial she had been living, but like her friends had.

"You should probably slow down on the drinks. I've never seen you drink this much. I wouldn't even know how to handle you if you got drunk."

Micah looked down at another empty glass. How many had it been? Who was counting, anyway? "Well, you're about to find out. I cannot be held responsible for my actions tonight."

"Oh, jeez."

"Hey, that girl over there keeps checking you out."

"Yeah. So?"

"So, I've seen you look at her, too. You should go talk to her."

"Can't. I'm talking to you."

"So I'm the lucky one tonight?"

"Guess so." His piercing gray eyes were trained on her. Evaluating her. She must have passed. "Wanna play a game?"

"A game?"

"Yeah. It's kind of a game."

"Like what?"

"Let's try and read people based off of what they're drinking."

She hoped he could read the perplexity on her face. Was he being serious?

"Come on. It will be fun."

"Okay. You start."

"Okay, see that guy over there? The one in the red shirt? Watch him. He was just looking at the list of margaritas, but put it away after he noticed the hot bartender. Fifty dollars says he orders whiskey straight."

"Oh, so now this is turning into a money game? Okay, you're on."

Micah watched as the bartender handed the man in the red shirt a shot glass filled with amber liquid. He sat it down in front of him, where it remained untouched.

"Why isn't he drinking it?"

"He can't handle it. That's why he was looking at the margarita list."

She rolled her eyes. *This is dumb.*

Josh took a long draw from his beer as a beautiful woman sauntered past their table, flashing him a come-and-get-me smile. Micah sat there with her mouth hanging open at the audacity of the woman. Was Micah really so irrelevant that the woman didn't consider her to be with Josh? She wasn't, but still. Seriously? Josh smiled back but moved on. His eyes moved back to the bar, past the man with the untouched shot of whiskey, scanning the other patrons.

"Okay, it's your turn."

"No. I'm not any good at this."

"Okay…see the bombshell at the end of the bar?" Micah's eyes narrowed as he accentuated the word *bombshell.* "She's been nursing that Corona for about half an hour now. She's alone, looking good and drinking light? I can almost guarantee that she has no intentions of leaving this bar alone tonight. She'll start throwing them back more heavily once some guy starts buying them for her. Then she'll pretend she doesn't want to go anywhere, but if some lucky guy reads the signs right he'll know that Miss Corona-with-Lime is ready to roll."

"You are crazy. Do you always do this?" She watched as he shrugged his broad shoulders and nursed his Sam Adams. "What about me? What do my drinks say?"

"Well…your drinks tell me a couple of things. One,

the variety of your drinks tells me that you steal people's drinks and don't pay for your own. And second, they say you won't remember any of what I just said, anyway."

"Well, then…why don't you go buy one for Miss Corona-with-Lime? She's already looked over here twice." She was feeling saucy tonight. Josh noticed. Quirked his eyebrow, and gave her a smile.

"Someone has to keep you from making bad decisions tonight."

"And you're volunteering?"

"For now. As soon as you start to drive me nuts, I'm bailing."

"Good to know I have such a great friend to count on in my time of need."

"Any time."

The alcohol was definitely starting to go to her head, making her feel all tingly and disjointed. Josh was starting to look a little hazy as he sat across from her giving her the most puzzling looks. He really was beautiful, reminded her of an iron sculpture in a way—masculine, rough, hard edges, but beautiful nonetheless. Even his eyes were metallic in essence: an odd shade of gray, sometimes taking on blue, sometimes green. Women seemed to love them. She found them piercing and cold. She had always preferred blue eyes, like Drew's were.

A vivid memory swept over her. She gulped down the last of her drink and signaled for another. Josh looked as if he was about to ditch her. "Don't leave me."

"Why?"

"I don't want guys bothering me."

"Oh, I wouldn't worry about that. They'll stay far away from you as long as you keep flashing that evil scowl. I think you are scaring everyone in this place, including me. I just need to get some water, and I have no idea where our waitress has run off to. I will be right back."

The more she drank, the more she remembered. The more she remembered, the more she drank, an endless cycle of tequila and haunting memories. She and Drew had been high-school sweethearts, planning on forever. She hadn't just lost her boyfriend that night. She'd lost the love of her life, the kids they would have had, the dream house and the hand that would have held hers as they grew old together. That accident had robbed her of her chance at happiness, stripped her of every dream and desire in one tragic move.

Oh, gawd. She was even starting to annoy herself. This was just pathetic. The tequila wasn't working. It was only making it worse.

"Micah, you're not looking so good."

Well, Josh, you are starting to look really good.

Oh, my! Where did that come from?

Josh's hand cupped her chin, lifting her face until she looked him in the eye. "How many have you had?"

"That's irrelevant. Do you know Drew would have been twenty-eight? Can you believe that?"

"Yeah. It's hard to imagine."

"It's like his image has been frozen in time. Forever eighteen."

"Come on. We need to get you home."

"I am fine, Josh. I am not drunk yet. I promise."

"Are you kidding me? You're wasted, like legit wasted. Can't believe I didn't stop you before now. You never drink. What's gotten into you?" His hand wrapped around her arm, urging her to stand and helping her into her coat.

She didn't get drunk. She was too much of a lady to act like the common drunken college students who littered this place. Then again, she had consumed a lot. Now that she thought about it, maybe she was drunk, because she could not remember just how many drinks she had had. The room tilted and she was forced to grab Josh for support. Maybe he was right. All she knew was her plan hadn't worked; she hadn't drunk enough to forget.

CHAPTER TWO

JOSH HAD TAKEN Micah all the way back to her apartment before realizing she had left her purse and keys at the bar.

"I just miss him so much, Josh." Micah had been talking like this since they left the pub. This new version of her was getting old fast. Thankfully, this was her first attempt at what he would classify as "escaping the pain." Although judging by her slurred words on the way home, it hadn't worked.

She wasn't in a good state of mind. It was time someone intervened. And as her best friend, it seemed the responsibility fell in his lap. But now wasn't the time. He'd talk to her tomorrow.

"I know. We all do."

"But you weren't going to marry him. I was. You weren't in love with him. Were you, Josh? I would understand if you were. He was gorgeous."

Where was this all coming from? She hadn't talked this way in years. Until recently, she had appeared normal. He'd never once wondered if she was still hung up on Drew. But since this anniversary started looming over her head, she'd become this depressing, weepy mess that everyone was getting tired of quickly.

"No. We were just friends, Micah. I prefer women."

He would just go with it for now. What else could he do at this point?

"Yeah, he preferred women, too…maybe too much. One time I caught him kissing another girl."

That was news to Josh. He had always suspected something, but never thought Drew would be stupid enough to cheat on Micah. Josh mentally cursed his dead friend.

"I always thought we would kiss. You know…you and me. Why haven't you ever kissed me?"

Josh's head jerked in Micah's direction, accidentally turning the wheel with him. They both whipped back and forth as he tried to get his truck under control.

"Whoa! I think I'm gonna be sick. Can you not drive so crazy?" She let her head fall back on the headrest and closed her eyes.

What the—? Did she just say what he thought she just said? His eyes kept going back and forth from the road to her.

She sat up again, her eyes big and round and full of sadness. "I just miss him so much, and no one else does. I just can't stand it anymore." Micah burst into tears. The mopey drunk had turned into a weepy drunk right in front of his eyes.

This was getting ridiculous. Okay, maybe it was far past that point already. Either way, he wasn't sure how much longer he could put up with this depressed version of his best friend. And where was this talk about kissing coming from? It all had caught him off guard.

Twelve years ago, when he first met Micah, she was this vibrant ball of fireworks, red hair blazing with the personality to match. After the accident, after they graduated high school, she had disappeared, too caught up in her grief to socialize much. It was understandable. They'd all felt the same way. When college came around, they were thrown together in some of the same courses, and the rest was history. He helped pull her from her despair even though she had never quite returned to her former self.

He turned to peek at her again. Okay, so maybe he was wrong. He hadn't cured her completely. His eyes briefly took in the tearstained cheeks before he turned his attention back to the road.

He needed to see her restored again. Not just to the way she had been these past ten years, but to the vibrant and feisty person she was before Drew.

It probably didn't help that she never dated. For a long time he'd thought maybe she was crushing on him, and now after her little confession… That was beside the point. *She's drunk. It's all nonsense.*

He parked the car, thankful that there was a spot close to the building. Micah was a weepy mess, forcing him to help her up the three flights of stairs. She owed him big!

He couldn't get to his keys, and every time he let go of her she started to fall over. Her body leaned heavily against his, her soft fragrance overwhelming his senses. Ever since she'd made that remark in the truck, he couldn't stop thinking about kissing her. By this point he was just flat-out frustrated. On *all* levels.

Putting his firefighter training to use, he flung her limp body over his shoulder, reached for his keys and opened the door. Yeah, he deserved a steak dinner after this…at the very least.

Finally getting into his bedroom, he wanted to throw her onto the bed. She was too far gone for it to bother her. She deserved the couch after the way she had been acting lately, driving everyone insane with her late-onset depression, but he couldn't bring himself to do that to her. She would have a killer hangover in the morning.

That was punishment enough for being such a pain in his butt lately.

His phone vibrated in his back pocket. Pulling it out, he saw Sabina's name on the top of the screen.

"Hey. Did you find her stuff?"

"Yeah. I've got it."

"She's already passed out at my place, so don't worry about getting it to her now."

"Is she going to be okay, Josh?" Sabina's voice was marked with concern, the same concern he had felt recently.

"I don't know. I hope so. It might be time for a harsh reality check if she doesn't get her act together soon."

"As tough as that sounds, I agree."

They said their goodbyes and hung up. Josh had a lot to think about tonight. How did he tell his best friend to quit being depressed? He knew he couldn't, but there had to be a way to help. Maybe after tonight she would be fine and he would never have to bring it up. At least that was what he was hoping for.

He looked back at her sleeping form as she lay on his bed. He sat down next to her and pulled her feet into his lap. She was wearing these ridiculous strappy heels that looked a little on the freaky side. He was sure they belonged to Sabina. Micah would never purchase something as complicated as these. It took him a moment, but he figured out how to unfasten each buckle and tugged them off her feet. He struggled with her in such a passed-out state, but he finally got her out of her jacket, too. He pulled the covers back and over her, tucking them close to her. He brushed the curls back from her face and took a moment to study her in such a rare, peaceful state.

"Why have you become so intent on holding on to a

ghost, Micah? Tell me that. When will you finally be free of him?"

Josh leaned forward and placed a soft kiss on her forehead. Tomorrow would be difficult, forcing her to face some hard truths. He hoped he would not lose his friend because of it. Oh, he prayed it would never come to that.

"Josh?" She sounded so small and fragile when she spoke.

"Yes?"

"Hold me."

He had always been putty in her hands, would do anything for her. Over the years, he had learned to control his feelings for her, to tamp down the desire he felt. It almost became easy after a while; dating other women helped refocus all of that pent-up energy, leaving him free to be what Micah needed him to be. But he was a man, after all, a red-blooded man, and his control could only withstand so much. Those two little words threatened to unravel years of hard work.

But how could he deny her? He leaned over her while his mind and body battled it out.

Her eyes slowly opened, the full force of her warm brown gaze hitting him hard. Her pink lips parted ever so slightly. She had no idea the seductive power she had over him.

"Why didn't you ever kiss me, Josh?"

Her words came out like a whisper, caressing his skin as he hovered over her.

"I always wanted you to." Desire coursed through him at the sound of her admission.

"I haven't been kissed since Drew. I haven't even been on a date, really. I don't count that guy I lost the bet to." Her voice held a sensual quality, washing over him, weak-

ening his resolve. "I don't need a man when I have you...
but I do *need* to be kissed."

There was too much at stake. He couldn't risk losing
her. He couldn't risk hurting her.

Her small hand reached up, cupped the side of his face.
He found himself leaning into it even as her hand moved
up and around his neck. He closed his eyes as her fingers
combed through his hair, not realizing until it was too
late that she was pulling him closer.

Her soft, tentative lips moved against his, leaving him
powerless. He responded to her kiss; the tiny thread on
which his control was hanging snapped in an instant.
Years of restrained passion ignited as he deepened the
kiss.

The ferocious intensity of the need he felt building
within caused him to rein it in. And as he did, sanity returned. He ended the kiss abruptly, realization dawning
on him. Micah's eyes were wide in shock, her breathing
ragged as she lay pinned beneath him. He looked down
to find his hand on her breast.

He muttered a curse as he jumped up from the bed
and left the room in a hurry. With the offending hand
clenched in a fist, he prayed she was too drunk to ever
remember what had just happened. It would ruin everything!

Micah lay there, stunned. The fog suddenly cleared. Time
had stopped. Her breathing halted, or maybe she was
breathing faster than normal. She couldn't tell.

She had been vaguely aware of Josh as his large frame
hovered over her, his face close to her own. She had seen
his tongue as it peeked out ever so slightly and wet his
lips. His gaze pinned to her mouth. Micah had acted on
instinct, not fully aware of her own actions.

Then, *bam!*

She wanted to blame it on her vivid imagination or her wasted mind-set. None of this was real, and that kiss…

Oh, that kiss! Her body was still humming from the intensity of that kiss.

No. There was no way her imagination could have come up with a kiss like that. Her rapidly beating heart spoke volumes in and of itself.

She felt so much at the moment: desire, heat and… guilt? Drew's face plastered at the forefront of her mind. Her stomach turned.

Micah's head decided it hurt too much to think right now. She longed for sleep and prayed good dreams would come and steal her from reality and the inevitable hangover that she was already dreading. Why did she think tequila had been a good idea in the first place?

Closing her eyes, she buried herself under the covers and let herself fall under the spell slumber provided.

The smell of fall surrounded her. Micah couldn't quite define it, but if she could bottle it she would. It was crisp and fresh and automatically brought images of falling leaves and apple picking. And no one did fall the way New England did. The air was just cool enough to require a jacket, but still nice enough that she and her friends could spend the evening outdoors.

Her hair whipped in the wind, and in this moment of sheer contentment, she allowed it. Pulling the tie from her hair, she let it go wild and free. Drew's beautiful blue eyes lit up as he watched.

"Oh, Micah O'Shea." His voice had a deep, grizzled quality as he said her name.

"What?"

"You know I love when you let your hair down."

His voice was just above a whisper as he reached out and grasped a piece between his fingers. "The color is breathtaking."

Her cheeks grew warm and she silently cursed herself for it. Her ivory skin had an awful habit of turning a splotchy shade of crimson at times. She could feel it happening now.

"Do you two always have to make googly eyes at each other like that?" Jamie's voice broke their little moment like a baseball bat connecting with crystal. That was Jamie.

"You're just jealous," Sabina chimed in from the tailgate of Jamie's pickup truck. That's what best friends were for—always had one another's backs.

"Thanks for the birthday dinner, guys. You didn't have to do that." Drew leaned back in the grass on his elbows and crossed his legs at the ankles.

"Yeah, right. You'd kick our butts if we didn't." Josh threw a football at Drew, forcing him to sit back up in a hurry. They all laughed at the truth of that statement. The six of them did everything together, therefore every birthday was mandatory.

Micah curled into Drew's side as he settled back in the grass. She loved listening to his laughter rumble deep in his chest every time the guys said something funny. He smelled like fresh laundry and his cologne. She had bought a small bottle of it and put some on the teddy bear he had won for her last year at the fair. She slept with it every night, breathing in his scent. She knew it was pathetic, and would be mortified if anyone ever found out.

The two of them remained that way until the sky grew dark. She loved looking at the stars, but tonight the sky was too cloudy to see anything but a dark midnight-gray sky.

"Is that a star?" He pointed straight up.

"Where? I think you're seeing things. I can't see anything."

"It probably isn't." His laugh rumbled beneath her.
She felt him kiss the top of her head. He was always doing
little things like that, small actions that made her feel
precious, loved. His hand gently rubbed back and forth
along her back. It was soothing. She could fall asleep
here in the grass, in his arms. She could spend forever
with him like this.

"I love you," she murmured into his neck.

"I love you, too."

They were completely lost in one another. Their
friends were still there, not paying any attention to them,
just as the two of them were not paying any attention to
the others. He lifted her hand from his chest and placed
a warm kiss to her palm, cradling it to his cheek. Yes,
she could stay like this forever.

The cool night air drifted over them. Everyone had become so quiet that it was easy to hear the leaves rustling
around them, the small town below them settling down
for the night. It was beautiful. Magical. It was a memory
that would forever be imprinted on her mind. Embraced
in the arms of the one she loved, surrounded by friends
who were always there—yes, a memory to last a lifetime.

She wasn't sure how long they were there. Time just
seemed to stop for the six of them. A tiny droplet hit
her forehead. At first, she wondered if it was from the
trees above them, but then another followed. The droplets grew in size and intensity, bringing an end to their
magical night.

Drew yelled his thanks to everyone as they all dashed
to their cars to escape the downpour. Micah ran to
Drew's car. She ducked down into the low seat as he
scrambled to the other side.

The October air was already crisp; the added rain only compounded the chill. She shivered and pulled her jacket tighter as Drew fumbled with the heat controls.

"It should warm up quickly." Drew maneuvered the car back to the road and headed in the direction of her house. She felt guilty that he had to take her all the way back to her house when his was right there, but he had insisted on driving her.

The rain was coming down in sheets, making it nearly impossible to see past the windshield. Suddenly she was worried about Drew. "Are you all right driving in this?"

"I'll be fine."

He reached out for her hand and gave her a look she knew well. "I could always stay the night, though."

"Yeah, my parents would love that."

"It was worth a try."

He pulled into her driveway and turned off the car. They sat there in silence for a while, neither one wanting to end the night. He still held her hand, pulling her closer as he went in for a kiss over the center console. She loved kissing him. He knew how to kiss, how to use his lips. Of course, she had nothing else to compare to, but she was positive he was one of the best. She didn't want to consider how he got so good, instead just reveled in the fact that she was the one he was kissing now.

His hand began to roam. She needed to get closer, needed more of him, but the console was in the way. Seriously?

He unzipped her jacket, his hand moving toward the hem of her sweater. It slipped under and his cool hands met her warm flesh. It felt good, too good. Red flags began to wave. Sirens began to sound.

No. Not yet.

"I told you already. I'm not ready. Why must you always push it?"

"I'm sorry. I just figured..."

"What? It's your birthday, so you can get away with it?"

"No..."

"Save it. Happy birthday, Drew." She opened the car door. Rain and cold air slapped her in the face. She ran toward the front porch, not looking back. She heard his car start again and the tires peeling out onto the road. She had made him mad, but oh well. He had made her mad, too. This conversation had become too familiar. She didn't understand why he kept pushing it.

CHAPTER THREE

A CONTINUAL THROB at her temples pounded out a beat any drum line would be proud of. The gentle sway back and forth had her wondering how she had ended up on a boat. Did she even know anyone with a boat?

Slowly, ever so slowly, she attempted to pry her eyes open. The stickiness proved that last night's choice to layer up the mascara and falsies had been a bad idea.

Drinking was not something she did regularly, and apparently should never do again. She was a mopey, pathetic drunk and in the morning she still felt...well, mopey and pathetic. So what was the point?

Micah was too afraid to open her eyes, not wanting to experience the piercing pain the bright morning light would bring.

Drew had visited her in her dreams and it made her feel as if she was seventeen all over again. It was as if the years that had passed had ceased to exist. No death, no pain. She didn't want to open her eyes and face the inevitable disappointment. But last night she'd made a promise to herself. This was going to stop. She needed to snap out of it.

With a groan, she rolled over and stretched. The fogginess slowly began to dissipate as she opened her eyes, leaving a clear view of...not her room. Gradually, she began to recognize her surroundings. She had helped pick out that mirror. And that dresser, too.

It was Josh's room.

The smell of tequila and smoke rose up from her clothes and memories of last night came crashing back as thoughts of her dream faded away.

Josh. She had kissed Josh.

The memory of his lips upon hers was permanently engraved in her brain. Who could forget a kiss like that? Whether she was drunk or not, those lips were unforgettable.

How embarrassing! She threw a pillow over her head. This couldn't be happening. What was she supposed to do? Apologize? Act as if it hadn't happened? Laugh it off? There had been a lot of alcohol involved. It could easily be swept under the rug.

The smell, coming from the clothes she had worn the night before, turned her stomach. She threw the covers aside and bolted from the bed, making a mad dash to the bathroom. Immediately, she hugged the porcelain bowl, cursing herself for last night's stupidity.

A soothing hand made circles on her back, easing some of the sickness.

"Good. You're awake."

Josh's voice was a balm to her frazzled state. Her head hurt too much to look up at him.

"Do you want me to get you anything?"

She couldn't summon the strength to answer.

"Sorry. I can't stay in here or else I'm going to be pushing you aside so that I can puke. Call me if you need something."

Minutes later, she finally pulled herself away from the toilet, having dispensed of everything and then some. Desperately needing water, she made her way to the kitchen. Josh had such a nice place for a guy. Of course, she had helped with most of it. He'd wanted the apartment to have a woman's touch without having to invest in a relationship that came attached to a woman.

As she rounded the corner to the kitchen, Josh came into view. Their gazes locked. An onslaught of images from last night's impromptu but very passionate kiss returned to the forefront of her mind. Heat rushed from her toes to the top of her head with lightning speed. She could feel the crimson flush as it stretched across her face, down her neck and across her chest.

Micah could see it in his eyes. He was thinking about the kiss, too. She should look away, but she couldn't. His steel-gray eyes held her captive. She allowed herself to break the eye contact for just a moment, taking in his fire-station tee and the way it left little to the imagination. Her eyes traveled back up to his and he quickly looked away.

He stood behind the black granite countertop making coffee, the delicious-smelling aroma pulling her from her overheated thoughts. Without having to ask, he handed her a cup as well as a bottle of water. He knew her so well.

"Sorry about last night." She cringed as the words spilled out of her mouth, her voice sounding more like a croak. *Sorry* seemed like such an inadequate word to cover all her transgressions. She was mortified at the boundaries she had crossed.

She sat at the kitchen table, her hands wrapped around the modern handleless coffee cup, and absorbed its warmth. Sending up a quick but heartfelt prayer, she hoped that her actions from last night had not done any permanent damage to their relationship.

"Don't mention it." He was busy with something in the kitchen, she couldn't tell what from her spot.

Micah tried to make sense of everything. Some fog-giness still resided from her drunken haze, clouding her mind. She struggled to separate dream from reality. But regardless, the kiss she'd initiated was bold and clear. Nothing about that was clouded.

"Why do you keep looking at me like that?" Josh snapped at her.

"Like what? I'm not looking at you."

"Yes, you are. It's weirding me out. Stop."

So he was going to avoid the issue at hand. Good. She didn't want to talk about it, anyway.

Plopping down across from her at the table, he poured half the box of cereal into what appeared to be a small mixing bowl.

"I have no idea what you are talking about. Jeez! You gonna save me any?"

"It's my cereal. I can eat it all if I want to."

"You'd do that to your guest?" Her head was pound-ing and this conversation wasn't helping. Eating might not be such a good idea, anyway.

"Guest? Um…you left me no choice. You were *oblit-erated* last night. If you hadn't lost your purse, I would have happily taken you to your own place."

She looked up from her coffee and immediately regret-ted the quick movement. The room began to spin again. She needed to lie back down, not argue about cereal.

It was his way of avoiding an embarrassing conversa-tion. The cereal was unimportant.

"You've got something—" He waved his hand over his cheek.

Puzzled, she waited for him to finish.

"You've got—" He reached out. Her body went rigid as his hand touched her cheek. Then he ripped something off her face. "It's an eyelash from last night."

After flicking the wayward false eyelashes onto the table, he turned his attention back to his cereal.

She was still locked out of her apartment, so this place would have to do for now, at least until this feeling of being on a rocking ship subsided.

"Josh, I need to lie back down. I don't feel so good." Her bare feet shuffled against the old hardwood floors as she made her way back to his room. The smell of last night's bar still clung to her shirt: the smoke, the booze, the other miscellaneous smells that went along with a pub. "And I'm stealing a T-shirt."

"Why not? You've taken over everything else."

Slipping out of her clothes, she pulled on a vintage band tee she found in his dresser, relishing in the way the cool cotton felt against her warm skin. She dove under the covers and buried her head in the pillow. The unsettling feeling of being surrounded by Josh washed over her, his scent clawing her senses. She had helped him pick out the fragrance, too. Even in her tequila haze she could easily pull out the notes of bergamot, Douglas fir and citrus. It was him, completely him.

Until now, she had not realized just how much his scent had affected her. Memory of last night's kiss teased her senses once again. She buried herself deeper, needing more of it, needing more of him.

When had this happened? When had she stopped looking at Josh as a friend or a brother? She was positive this kind of traitorous behavior was punishable by death. One did not simply move on from a deceased boyfriend to his best friend, even if a significant amount of time had passed. And it definitely wasn't wise to start feeling this kind of desire for a man who thought of you as a sister.

Although that kiss said differently. Sleep claimed her before she was able to analyze and gain answers to the questions that now troubled her.

Josh had been worried about her last night. Micah tended to bottle her emotions until the contents were so compressed that the explosion that followed was a grand display of red flames and fireworks.

And that was exactly what he got. He just hadn't expected it to be in the form of an earth-shattering kiss. A huge part of him wanted to smile, to relish in the excitement of finally being able to kiss the one girl who had always been out of his reach. But the moment he allowed that excitement to build, it was swallowed up by betrayal and guilt.

She had been drunk out of her mind. He thought for sure that she wouldn't remember a thing, but he had been wrong. She remembered all right, judging by the way her face had turned a beautiful shade of pink when she saw him.

It had been a mistake.

The grief she had been experiencing recently was bound to make her do something stupid and out of control. Clearly that was what had happened last night.

But if that had been the result of her depression, enough was enough. He couldn't stand any more of this. He should have talked with her sooner, done something sooner. But what? What did you tell your best friend who after ten years fell back into mourning the loss of her boyfriend? If there was a self-help book, he would have bought it by now. He hated seeing her unhappy, but she was her own worst enemy. She was the one keeping herself from happiness—real happiness, not the contrived happiness she had been living with for the last decade. She was only fooling herself. She deserved more than this.

And he definitely couldn't handle this latest development. He was wound too tight.

When she'd walked into the kitchen this morning with her rumpled clothes, her curls going in every direction and a false eyelash stuck to her cheek, everything in him had wanted to continue what they had started the night before.

The moment her eyes met his and he felt the embarrassment she felt, he'd known he was being foolish. It could never, ever happen. He set his mind back on course, but the frustration and tension were too difficult to ignore. Instead of pushing her against the counter and kissing her the way he wanted to, he'd snapped at her and argued over cereal.

Josh shook his head. Apparently, this was how he was going to handle this situation: by being a grouch and pissing her off. *Great idea, Josh. Real brilliant.*

The image of Micah's flaming hair spread out on his pillow left him breathless. Add in the fact that she was wearing his T-shirt and he was positive this had to be the most beautiful sight he had ever seen. He could feel the desire begin to take form deep in his gut as an intense urge pulled him closer. His hand moved on its own accord, desperate to touch the flames. If he touched would he get burned?

Josh yanked his hand back from her. Of course he would! Last night was proof enough for him. He was definitely playing with fire here.

He turned to leave, having done was he was supposed to and checked on her, making sure she was still breathing.

"Josh?"

Her sleepy voice almost did him in. Standing at the doorway with his back to her, he answered, "Yes?"

"What time is it?"

He found himself turning at the question. She rolled over in the bed and pushed her hair out of her face. He glanced at his watch. "A little after two."

"Two in the afternoon?" She sat up in the bed, her curls in wild disarray, making her impossibly irresistible. He could not stand to look at her anymore, so he turned back and headed in the direction of the living room.

"Yup. You slept the day away. You want anything to eat? I just ordered a pizza."

"Sounds good."

He flipped on the TV, hoping to find something to distract him, but it wasn't working. Micah helped herself to some water and came to sit next to him on the couch. He was aware of every move she made, every fidget, every sigh.

She wanted to talk. That much was obvious. But what was he supposed to say? In one stupid moment of weakness, he had brought about a whole new world of awkwardness between them. He'd really screwed this one up. Now he couldn't look at her without seeing her eyes wide in shock and horror, her lips raw from his kiss. The mere task of sitting within two feet of one another on a couch watching television had adopted all sorts of new complications. Ten years of hard work thrown out the window in an instant.

He had to figure out some way to control the damage he had done. Ignoring it, as if it hadn't happened, could only last so long. She would bring it up eventually. He needed to have a plan in place for when she did.

"So…"

She let the word stretch out, accentuating the resounding discomfort that sat between them.

Well, that didn't last long. *Don't go there, Mike. Don't go there.*

"That kiss last night..."

She went there.

"And I thought *I* was the one who had too much to drink! Ha! No one was paying any attention to *you.* I had no clue you got that handsy when you drank."

What? He'd only had one drink last night, but he wasn't about to correct her. It would be so easy to blame it on the alcohol.

"You do always leave the bar with a girl. Never thought I would be added to that never-ending list of hookups." She laughed again. There was an unmistakable pit in his stomach brought on by guilt.

"Obviously, we both had a little too much to drink. Honest mistake." *Stop talking, Mike.* The look he sent her said as much.

"Okay, fine. I'll drop it. It will be our little secret. Never to be talked about again. No one ever has to know. It will be like it never happened."

He narrowed his eyes, but didn't even have to look at her for her to get the point.

"Yeah. Sorry."

Hopefully that would be the last time it was brought up. They had talked about it, gotten it out in the open. Good enough. Right?

She kept fidgeting. She tucked her feet under her and turned in his direction. Every inch of him was aware of every minute move she made. At least he should be grateful she had stopped talking.

"I had the weirdest dream last night..."

Josh released a deep sigh as he continued to flip

through the channels, not really seeing what was flashing before him on the screen. He needed to get her home.

"Okay, fine. I won't tell you about it."

Now he was making her mad again. He was on a roll.

"No. Tell me."

"I was just trying to start a conversation. You know I can't handle awkward silences. Are you in a bad mood or something?"

"No."

The silence that stretched between them was uncomfortable, and, well, excruciatingly painful. Minutes later she let out a frustrated sigh.

"I need a shower. Do you mind?"

Of course I mind! I don't need any visuals of you in my shower!

Too late. The visuals were already there.

"Go ahead. Towels are in that small closet in the hall."

He tried not to map out her movements based on the sounds coming from the bathroom, but no amount of control could stop his mind from picturing the hot water washing over her porcelain skin. The kiss from the night before had set this runaway train in motion. It was impossible to stop it now.

He shook his head to clear the image, but it was only replaced by another when he heard the water shut off. She had to be drying off at this point. How could he have fallen so far as to be envious of a drop of water or even a towel?

Stop now! This was dangerous territory. Frustration built at his obvious lack of self-control when it came to his thoughts concerning Micah. It threatened to boil over as she stepped out of the bathroom, a cloud of steam surrounding her.

She wore nothing but a towel wrapped around her

decadent body, tiny droplets of water beaded on her still-damp skin. Half-dressed women had never affected him quite the way Micah did now. The ravenous hunger within him was like nothing he had ever experienced before. The need to kiss and taste the skin where her dripping hair clung to her damp shoulders overwhelmed him.

"Josh?"

The sound of his name snapped him back to his senses. He had momentarily been lost in steam and water droplets, staring at her like a starved and thirsty man. He was neither and she needed to go. Far away from him. And now.

"Seriously? Micah, put some clothes on!" Okay, so maybe that came out a little more forcefully than he had planned. He mentally added *jerk* to his growing list of attributes: disloyal, guilty, betrayer.

She stomped back into his bedroom, only to return wearing last night's clothes. Her wet hair left damp spots on the shoulders of her top.

"What are you doing?"

"I'm leaving."

"C'mon, Micah. You don't have to go. Sabina doesn't get off work until later." He really did feel bad for snapping at her.

"I can't handle being cooped up in this apartment for another second. You're being all cranky and whatnot. And, well, I don't have to put up with it."

She pulled the wet strands of her hair up and secured it with an elastic, put on her shoes and grabbed her coat. "Call me when your cycle is over and we can be friends again."

Without moving from his place on the couch, he watched as her fleeting figure disappeared. And just like always, she left a gaping Micah-shaped hole in her wake.

* * *

Micah stormed from the apartment building and out into the bright light of day. Ah, she wished she had her purse! Sunglasses would have been nice. Oh, and money. She was not going anywhere without that. Thank God she still had her phone in her back pocket, otherwise this would be a serious disaster. She called Sabina, not really expecting an answer. She never answered while at a photo shoot.

"Hello?"

"Oh, thank God!" Micah breathed a deep sigh of relief. "I can't handle Josh for another moment. He's driving me insane. When will you be done with your shoot?"

"I have a break now. I can come get you if I hurry. Where are you?"

"Outside Josh's building."

"Okay. I'll be there soon."

You could not get anywhere *soon* in Boston, but at least she now had a way home.

Her eyes scanned the busy street as she pulled her coat up higher on her neck. The chill of October in Boston was seeping in through her jacket. Buildings surrounded her except for one solitary tree forcing its way into a concrete world. Its leaves had started to change, a bright golden-yellow providing a stark contrast amid the dark grays of the city.

She still couldn't shake what had just happened between her and Josh. Not that she could figure out any of it. At first she had thought the chemistry that exploded between them was mutual, but after the way he was acting, she knew she had imagined that. How stupid could she be? She was far from the kind of girl he was attracted to. He saw her as a sister, for crying out loud! They were best friends! Crossing over that boundary had been a monumental mistake.

She had tried to brush it off as a joke, tried to ease the moment and laugh it off. But he was in such a bad mood she'd needed to get out of there quick. She needed to put some space between them in order to salvage their friendship. Hopefully after a day or two the kiss would be long forgotten and their friendship restored.

After what felt like forever, Sabina's SUV came into view as she maneuvered her way across lanes to stop outside Josh's apartment building. Micah quickly jumped into the car so that Sabina wouldn't be blocking traffic for too long. "Thank you. Thank you. Thank you. I don't know what I would have done if you hadn't been able to come!"

"What happened with Josh?"

"You know...Josh just being Josh."

"Say no more. Know exactly what you mean. He can be such a pain in the butt."

After Sabina dropped her off at their apartment, Micah changed and climbed into the comfort of her bed. She rolled over onto something and reached under the covers to find the teddy bear Drew had given her.

In the chaos surrounding the kiss, she had forgotten all about the dream. It had all seemed easier when Drew was still alive. Maybe all these new feelings for Josh were just misdirected emotions and longings. Maybe it was just her heart's way of searching for Drew and instead finding Josh.

Why did everything have to be so complicated?

Happiness had come naturally back then, but it had been a long time since she had felt that way. She wanted it back. Part of her still wanted Drew back. Obviously that was impossible, but last night's dream had been close.

She swiped her finger across her phone screen and saw a text message from Josh.

I'm such a jerk. Sorry <3

It would be easy to respond, but instead she clicked her phone off.

Micah was exhausted. These last couple months had taken her on an emotional roller coaster, but none of that had prepared her for the last twenty-four hours.

She had been depressed and tired of it. She wanted to finally face the past head-on and put it behind her once and for all. But last night's kiss coupled with the vivid dream that had brought all these memories back to the surface were all too much to handle.

Drew was an important part of her past. Josh was an important part of her present. Both were intricately woven into the tapestry of her life. But the question that remained was, what about her future?

CHAPTER FOUR

SHE HAD DREAMED of Drew again, but just as he would lean in to kiss her, the dream would suddenly change.

"Josh." Even saying his name aloud in the quietness of her room ignited something unfamiliar within her. She had joked about the kiss with him the day before, even going so far to blame it on him. She'd wanted to give the situation some levity, but it was proving to be far more serious than she thought. And Josh was taking up a good portion of her mind.

The two men had taken over her every waking and sleeping thought. She would wake up, perspiration beading on her brow as she shook the images of last night's dream from her mind.

She was holding firm to the notion that they were connected. If she cleansed herself of one problem, the other would fix itself.

Every year for the last ten years she had allowed herself a short time of grieving. This year was not shaping up to be quite what she had anticipated. This had to stop. She had to get control of this. No more moping. No more sadness. She would rid herself of her past once and for all.

She got out of bed and opened her closet door. Reaching up, she pulled down a bulky, heavy box. It was a box she rarely opened anymore, but had been in her possession for the last ten years. As she lifted the lid, the smell of old things drifted through the air as easily as the sense of nostalgia enveloped her.

Memories. Her memories.

Even as she had every intention of going through the box to put an end to this madness, she found herself desperate to cling to the memories. She had loved him deeply. Something like that could not just be tossed aside.

As she lifted an old photograph, she held it to her chest, wanting to grasp any part of Drew that she could. She couldn't throw any of this away. Not yet.

Time had seemed to wash out the memories, causing them to fade ever so slightly, but opening this box erased all the damage time had done.

She had forgotten so many things about him. Even the pain of losing him had dimmed. She could no longer remember his voice or the expressions of his face. But her fragmented dreams had brought it all back.

Lovingly, she lifted out his sweatshirt. The deep red color brought a different kind of sadness. She ran her fingers across the white letters stitched on the front—Harvard.

He'd had such dreams, such potential. He might not have ever been accepted into Harvard, but she did not doubt that he would have been successful wherever he ended up.

Putting the sweatshirt aside, she lifted out a stack of photos. Next, she pulled out a stack of letters. Long before text messages and email, handwritten notes and letters had existed, and they were sacred to her. She missed getting them.

Her eyes scanned each one, taking in the way he drew a heart in one fluid stroke of his pen. She had never seen anyone else do it that way. It made him unique.

Josh suddenly came to mind.

Now the man of her past and the man of her present dueled for a place in her heart. But the harsh reality of it was that she would lose this battle no matter what. She would never be able to have either one.

Micah took her time going through the box, reading each letter, staring at each picture, memorizing every detail. Then she put her favorite picture and her favorite letter aside. Everything else went back in the box and the lid back on top.

It was time. She had had her cry, and now it was time to move forward.

She carried the heavy box out to the living room and set it near the door. It was time for it to go. That was the healthy thing to do.

Sabina entered the apartment with her arms full of groceries and almost tripped over the box. She had obviously gone to the market and purchased a load of fresh fruit and vegetables. What really stuck out to Micah, though, were the flashy sequined top, black leather leggings and stilettos Sabina wore.

Sabina's eyes filled with worry as she took in Micah's tearstained cheeks and puffy red eyes, but thankfully she said nothing. Micah didn't want to talk about it just yet.

"You wore that to the market?"

"I ran out of clean clothes."

"You're kidding me, right?"

"No. What's wrong with this?" Sabina looked down at her outfit, trying to figure out what was wrong with it and seemingly forgetting she was still holding several bags of food.

"Here, let me help." Micah relieved her of some of the bags. "And let me inform you what is wrong with your outfit. No one wears sequins to the market, much less Marc Jacobs stilettos."

"I can. I have always said it is better to be overdressed than underdressed." Sabina gave Micah's look a once-over. "Besides, since when did the pajama queen start handing out fashion advice? Have you been sleeping all day again?"

"This isn't about me. Don't try to change the subject. Yes, you do always say that. But if you show up wearing a ball gown next week while trying to buy fresh fish, everyone will make fun of you."

"No, they won't. Everyone will just start wearing gowns the following week. I am a trendsetter."

Micah rolled her eyes. *A trendsetter, my butt.*

"And Mike, the fact that you knew these were Marc Jacobs did not escape my notice. It warms my heart."

Oh, yay! Just what she always hoped she would be capable of doing—spotting and naming designers at the drop of a hat.

"How did we become friends again?"

Josh needed to see her. There was this nagging emotion that had been plaguing him. He'd thought it would all go back to normal after a good night's sleep. That soon this would all be water under the bridge.

She never texted him back. He hadn't heard from her at all. Out of desperation, he texted Sabina, a rarity in and of itself, to check in on Micah. According to Sabina, she had slept the day away and appeared to have been crying. It was getting worse, not better. But the question was, did he step in to help, or did he give her space?

Maybe space was needed. She needed to work through these unresolved issues with Drew and he needed to get himself under control. Space was a good thing. At least that was what he kept telling himself.

Regardless, they needed to talk, clear the air. Then space could be possible, and at least his mind would be at ease. But as he stood at her doorstep, he realized he probably should have rehearsed what to say beforehand. He'd just have to see how it went.

He lifted his hand and placed three quick knocks on the hardwood door. A few moments later, the knob turned and door opened. Micah stood in front of him, appearing very much like the best friend he knew and loved in her oversize T-shirt and what she called comfy pants, her glasses in place and hair wadded up on top of her head. Her eyes were a little puffy and red, evidence of the tears Sabina had told him about.

She didn't say anything, just stood in the doorway, looking at him.

"I need to ask you something." The look she gave him told him it was okay to proceed. "How much do you think a polar bear weighs?"

She gave him a puzzled but knowing look. She knew him too well to know it wasn't a serious question plaguing his mind. "I don't know. How much?"

"Enough to break the ice." It got the response he wanted. Well, almost. It was a smile, even if forced. She moved aside to let him enter.

"I can't talk right now, Josh."

"You know, I used to have a pet porcupine."

"What? What in the world does that have to do with me not wanting to talk?"

"Oh, I'm sorry. I just thought we were beginning this conversation with each of us saying things that don't matter."

Her smile stretched from ear to ear. It didn't matter

what was going on between them. She could be mad at him and ready to spit fire his way, but he would saunter in and say something charming. What could he say? He had a way about him. It worked every time.

"Okay. I'll stop." He threw his hands up in surrender. "I just wanted to check in on you."

"As you can see, I'm fine." She extended both of her arms out in an effort to show she was in fact just fine.

"Are you sure about that?"

She didn't answer. Just sat down on the couch and stared at her hands.

"Micah, I hate seeing you hurt like this."

"I'm fine. Really. We don't need to talk about it."

"I knew you would say that." That was exactly what he expected from her. "But I'm kind of tired of waiting for the right time to talk to you."

She looked up with him, her eyes stretched wide. "I don't want to talk about it!"

"When will be the right time?" Recently his patience had been wearing thin, making him unsure of how to proceed, how to act around her, talk to her. It was all so exasperating. He had to remind himself to continue to be patient with her. She was in a delicate state of mind.

"I don't know. Maybe never."

She was frustrated and he knew it by the tone of her voice, the rigidity in her body language, but he wasn't about to give up on it so easily.

"Well, that doesn't work for me." Okay, handling delicate situations wasn't something that came easily for him. "You have to get over him."

Her gaze snapped back up at him as if he had taken her by surprise. Did she think he was talking about something else? Was she thinking about the kiss instead?

Her hesitation was clear. He could sense she was

searching for a response. He had definitely caught her off guard. Moments passed before she finally spoke.

"You...you say that like it's an easy thing. You don't know what it's like."

"You know you weren't the only one to go through this, right, Micah?"

He could see the anger stirring in her eyes, her feisty personality wanting to tell him off.

"No, but my relationship with him was different. My grief is different than yours. I can't tell you how to handle it any more than you can tell me how to handle mine."

"I'm not telling you how to grieve. I have kept silent. I have let you handle it your way. I've been there as a shoulder to cry on more times than I can count. I knew you needed time. But it has been *ten years*. You can't keep this up. What you are experiencing now is way past the point of being unhealthy."

"Unhealthy?"

"Yeah. You've taken grieving to a whole new level, and you were only with the guy for two years. Don't you think you've cried enough tears over him?"

Immediately, he regretted it. He had seen the pain in her eyes just before she turned her face from him. He knew better.

"I'm sorry. I shouldn't have said that." He stood in front of her and reached for her hand, pulling her up toward him. "Come here."

She came freely, tucking her head under his chin, resting her head on his chest. He knew the moment he pulled her closer that it was a mistake. Her warm body flush against his was wrong on so many levels. He pushed past it. She needed a friend instead of the jerk he had been recently.

She didn't say a word. She wasn't going to make it easy for him.

"Micah, if you keep going the way you've been, I fear you'll be just as dead on the inside as Drew's body in the grave."

Still no response.

She felt right in his arms. Like home. He couldn't lose her. He wanted to keep her safe, right where she was, close to his heart. Keep her safe from the pain of the world and the pain of her past. But he knew he needed to let go and let her do what she needed to do. He needed to support her and encourage her to move on, even if it meant she moved on from him, too. Because when you loved someone, you put their happiness above your own.

"I'm sorry. I didn't mean to hurt you."

"I know." She pulled back from him enough to look up into his face. "Why were we fighting in the first place, anyway? I was a little hungover, in case you forgot. I can't really remember what happened."

Relief coursed through him. There was hope. Maybe she wasn't thinking about the kiss after all.

"I don't know. I never know why we bother fighting. We both know there's no point to it. We're bound for life. It's inevitable. Nothing will ever come between us. I promise."

"Good. Because I can't imagine life without you." She pulled away from him completely and headed toward the door. "Can you do me a favor?"

She lifted up a worn-out old box and handed it to him. "Will you get rid of this for me?"

"Sure. What is it? Do you want me to donate it or toss it?"

"It's just some Drew memorabilia. I felt like it was about time I got rid of it."

He hadn't been prepared for that. Maybe she was moving on quicker than he had realized. "Really? Are you sure about that?"

"Didn't you just lecture me on this? Yes, I need it to be gone."

"Don't you want to hold onto some of it?" This was a big deal, especially for her.

"I already pulled out my favorites. The rest can go."

"Okay, but only if you're sure about it."

"I am."

He hadn't expected a change this quickly. She seemed to be handling it just fine.

"Hey, I have an idea..."

"What?"

"What if we both get a tattoo? You know, like in memory of..."

"You and your tattoos."

"But I'm serious. It will be fun. Plus, it will be something you have that will always remind you of him, but never take up valuable space in your closet."

She laughed, and then appeared to be contemplating his suggestion. He waited as she pondered.

"Okay. Let's do it."

"Awesome! I'll call my guy and you think about what you want to get."

Micah already knew what she wanted to get. She didn't need to think too hard on that one. This whole conversation, however, was something else entirely.

She thought he had been talking about the kiss! She had been sitting there mentally preparing herself for the awkward conversation, and he'd thrown her a curveball.

All this time she had thought her friends had considered her annual time of grieving as a minor inconvenience. Sure, she had just come to grips with her own denial of the situation, but she hadn't realized that Josh had noticed. She'd thought she was in control of it, the way she went about her life in a seemingly *healthy* manner, only allowing herself one period of time a year to cry. That was normal, right?

So maybe it wasn't. She had some issues to work through and she would. But never, ever had it crossed her mind that Josh had been aware of it.

Now she found out the truth! Had she always been so clueless? Did all of her friends think the same way Josh did? Did he really see her as someone who had unresolved grief issues? Did he really see her as such an unstable, unhealthy individual?

It was infuriating! All of her hard work over the years had been for nothing. The carefully placed mask had fooled no one but herself.

Argh! She wanted to scream!

CHAPTER FIVE

MICAH HAD BEEN avoiding him for almost a week now. She wouldn't take his calls and responded to his texts with one-word answers. Finally he just stopped trying to talk to her. Obviously, she had changed her mind after their talk the other day. What happened to "I can't imagine life without you"?

Had she been serious when she told him she needed space last week? He was so confused. If she wanted space, he would give it to her. But what if she needed a friend more and just didn't realize it?

Things had been slow lately at work, which at a fire station was a really good thing, except for the fact that it gave him more time to think about Micah and wonder what she was up to. They had been friends forever. Rarely had a day passed in the last several years that they didn't talk to one another. It was just how their relationship worked. Best friends. Always.

Josh had the day off, so after calling up Jamie, he decided to head up to his place for a long overdue visit to the farm. He knew after Jamie had cut out early the other night that this anniversary had been hard on him, too.

Drew and Jamie had been cousins, but acted more like brothers. He knew it was hard on Jamie, but the man refused to talk about it. Talking about his emotions was just something Jamie would never do, not that Josh would ever force him. Two men talking about their feelings could get real uncomfortable, real fast. But helping him out at the farm for the day would at least show him he cared. That was enough. At least he hoped it would be.

Josh took the longer way around the city to avoid traffic and headed north. Jamie's family farm was almost an hour outside of the city. Just close enough to enjoy the city, but far enough away to enjoy the country. That's just how Jamie liked it. None of it appealed much to Josh, though. He preferred the hustle and bustle of Boston. He wouldn't trade it for anything. But he had to admit, it sure was pretty this time of year.

Jamie's house was surrounded by heavily wooded areas, all painted in the shades of fall. The trees grew tall, arching over the road Jamie lived on. Micah would have loved taking this drive and seeing all the leaves changing colors. Man, that girl had a way of creeping back into his thoughts.

He shook his head, clearing his mind as he turned down the long driveway to Jamie's house at the back of the property. The heads of horses and other random farm animals popped over the fences to check out their visitor. The smell smacked him in the face long before he parked the truck and got out.

"How do you handle this smell?"

"It's nice to see you, too!" Jamie laughed as he came out the front door and stood on the deck. His flannel shirt, torn and dirty, showed he had already put in a lot of work today.

"How are you doing, man?"

"Good. You?"

"Doing all right. No complaints. Thought I'd come help you out today. Get my mind off some stuff."

"Sure. Could always use some help."

They fell into an easy rhythm feeding the animals and cleaning out stalls. There wasn't any reason to talk, but for some reason Josh couldn't help himself. "Micah was really upset you left early the other night."

"Yeah. Sorry about that. Figured it was time we all moved on, anyway."

"Yeah. We were thinking the same thing."

"Is she doing okay? Every time any of you bring her up, you sound worried. I haven't really talked to her in forever. I feel kind of guilty."

"We've all been worried, but then she woke up one morning last week and seemed over it. Now I can't get her to return my calls."

Jamie stopped what he was doing and looked at Josh.

"What?" Josh stopped as well and leaned on the pitchfork he was using.

"Is she dating?"

"Don't know." His shoulders moved up and down in a careless shrug. "Sabina insinuated that she was going to be setting her up."

"And how does that make you feel?"

"Seriously? You gonna go all Dr. Phil on me?" Josh dug the pitchfork back into the hay, this conversation passing the point of ridiculous.

Jamie laughed and went back to work. "Don't need to. You just told me all I needed to know."

"What are you talking about?" He stopped again. The horse in the stall next to them peeked over as if curious about Jamie's response as well. He had been right—when men talked about their feelings, it got awkward.

"You have feelings for Micah."

"Wha—?" Josh was dumbfounded. "No way."

Jamie continued his work, moving on to the next stall,

while Josh just stood there speechless, the horse nudging him with its nose. Josh ignored the horse, too caught up in Jamie's words.

"You're jealous. That is what you are currently feeling, but too dense to realize. Sabina tells you she's setting Micah up on some dates, and you got jealous."

"What are you talking about?"

"It's all over your face, not to mention the fact that you only come to visit me when something is bothering you."

"I do not."

"Stop lying to yourself."

"I can't have feelings for Micah."

"Why not?"

"Because she belongs to Drew. That's why."

"She *belonged* to Drew. Past tense."

"He may be gone, but one, she is obviously still in love with him and hung up on him. And two, he was one of my best friends. That's like breaking some kind of bro code."

Jamie shook his head. "Sounds like a bunch of excuses to me."

Micah was on the road to recovery. Finally. She had a plan in place and would have this conquered in no time. First things first. Her job.

She had worked as a nanny since she was in college. It was comfortable. It represented complacency and security, things that no longer had a place in her life. So she quit.

She had a business degree. It was time to put it to use. After a quick call to Hanna, who used her connections, Micah scored a great interview.

Her second part of the plan was to start taking better care of herself. It was time to get rid of the ice cream.

No more crying into a tub of chocolate with marshmallow swirl.

She was also in desperate need of a haircut, and maybe even a little update to the wardrobe. Sabina went shopping with her and helped her out. She fought past the urge to reject every suggestion her roommate gave her, but she had to face the truth. The girl was doing something right, and maybe, just maybe, some of that might rub off onto Micah.

It felt good, as though she was recapturing some of her old self little by little.

Micah used her knee to bang on the door of Josh's apartment. It was Sunday, which meant an afternoon of football and food with her friends. She had spent the last few days avoiding Josh, but it was time to face him. She couldn't ignore him forever.

The girls were responsible for the food this week and somehow she had gotten saddled with the task of picking it all up. Her arms were heavy-laden with the grocery bags, as she hadn't wanted to take more than one trip up three flights of stairs.

Jamie answered the door. "Oh, hey! Let me help you with that. Why didn't you call? I would have come down and grabbed them for you."

"You know I like to pretend I'm fiercely independent." He transferred the bags from her arms to his as she shut the apartment door.

Micah entered the living room area and saw Josh sitting on the couch, with his three-year-old niece cuddled up on his lap. She wasn't prepared for the rush she felt at seeing him again. She had told herself her initial reaction the other night had been completely imagined. After one too many drinks, she had misconstrued an accidental brush of lips and made it in to something more. There was no way she felt anything more than friendly toward Josh. The only emotion she was currently feeling was irritation or frustration or something like that.

Yeah, right. Keep telling yourself that.

She took in his hair, purposely tousled in its usual fashion, and the color of his shirt, which made his eyes stand out even more. Everything she had just told herself had been a lie.

You might be a little out of practice, but this is lust, honey. Pure and simple. Now wipe the drool and smile like you mean it.

His face lit up when he saw her enter the room. "Hey."

Suddenly she didn't know how to act around him. Smiling was not as easy as it once had been. She now knew what it felt like to have those lips on hers.

Instead, she focused on his niece. She could do this.

"Lily, I didn't know you were going to be here today." The little girl turned to her and her face lit up. She jumped off his lap and ran over to Micah. She picked her up and gave her a big bear hug. "Is your mommy here, too?"

"No, Unca Joshie watchin' me."

"Oh, well, that's fun."

Josh stood up and walked over to her to grab the remaining grocery bag. "Here, let me."

He tried to take the bag, but Lily wanted her uncle back and lunged toward him. He abandoned the bag and caught her just in time, leaving Micah awkwardly grasping at both the girl and the bag wedged between them.

"Silly girl." He placed a raspberry on Lily's cheek before turning his attention back to Micah. Once he had the little girl in check, he grabbed hold of the remaining groceries with his free hand.

His eyes seemed to question her, gauge how she was

doing, but she seemed to pass inspection. "What are we having today?"

"All kinds of goodies." *Breathe, Micah.* One kiss and suddenly she could no longer function. Apparently the frustration she'd felt had overshadowed this new emotion the other day when he came over. She might need to find something to get angry about again.

"Looking forward to it."

Micah headed to the kitchen and began to organize everything to make quick work of the food preparation. Josh stood in the kitchen, making it seem much too small all of a sudden. He drew close and peeked over her shoulder to see what all she had.

He was so close she could smell him, feel the heat radiating off his body. Lily's giggle broke her spell.

"Let's see what she's got here, Lily."

"Ooh! Chips!"

"You want some?" Micah opened the bag and held it out for the little girl. Lily grabbed a handful, which with her tiny chubby fingers meant two. Kind child that she was, she shared with her uncle, feeding a chip to him. He opened wide, pretending he was a monster devouring the chip. She giggled and fed him the other chip, too.

"You're gonna give Joshie all your chips?"

"He's hungry monstah."

"Well, then you need to keep feeding him." She handed Lily a couple more chips.

"No. You feed him!" Lily, with a big smile on her face, pushed the chips back at Micah. "I scared."

Scared? Yeah, you and me both, kid! Josh looked at her over Lily's head, mouth wide open, waiting to be fed a chip. Micah placed the chip in his mouth, her fingertips grazing his lips. Something flared in his eyes, but quickly disappeared. Instead he winked at her as he chomped down on the chip. *Monstah,* indeed.

"Now get out of here, you two. I have some food to prepare." She balled up her tingling fingertips before trying to shake the feeling from them. *Snap out of it!*

Hanna arrived a few minutes later and together they were able to get lunch and snacks going quickly. The game had started already and the boys were watching while the girls remained in the kitchen.

"Whoa! Whoa! Whoa! What was that? Come on, ref!"

"Unbelievable!"

The guys were shouting and yelling at the television as if the referees could hear them. The same thing happened every week. It was typical guy behavior during a football game. Josh was on his feet, one arm raised in the air as he accentuated his words to the referees, while the other arm had a giggling Lily in a football hold.

Micah smiled to herself.

"You would think with three of us against the two of them, we wouldn't have to watch football every Sunday," Sabina complained as she gnawed on a carrot stick.

"Oh, come on. It's a tradition we've had every season for as long as I can remember," Hanna defended.

"Yeah, and baseball, basketball and hockey, too."

"Well, it comes with living in Boston. We love our sports."

"While we are on the subject of traditions, I think we have too many. We need to reconsider some of them."

"What's wrong with traditions?" Micah felt a little offended by Sabina's comments. They always had fun no matter what they did together. Although, she was sure there would be complaints if they started attending fashion shows and operas.

"No need to get defensive. Jeez! I was only stating my

opinion. Don't worry. I don't think any of your precious traditions will be messed with."

"Hey, is the buffalo-chicken dip finished?" Hanna had her arms full of chips to take out to the guys.

"Just about. You can take the veggies and dip, if Sabina would stop eating all of them. Oh, and the pizza bites are ready, too."

"No wonder I can't stick to my diet." Hanna rolled her eyes.

"Yeah, you and me both."

"Oh, I love when you girls are in charge! We get the best football food."

"How about you guys pick something different than pizza next week?"

"Like what? Calzones? Hey, Josh, we can go to that place around the corner. That chick was really diggin' me last time." Jamie stuffed his face with a chip overloaded with buffalo-chicken dip.

"Yeah, right. She was so into *me*. Even gave me her number."

"Seriously?" Jamie's brow furrowed as he sat forward and looked at Josh.

Josh nodded, showing he was participating in the conversation, but the whole time he was playing a staring game with Lily. She sat on his lap, her little hands framing his face, her forehead resting on his. It was the cutest scene, but nothing new to Micah. Josh had always been like this with his nephews and nieces. Unca Joshie was the best.

"Can't believe it. I thought she was hitting on me! Man, I was really into her, too."

"You want her number?" Josh ended the staring game, kissing Lily on the nose. She let out another string of giggles.

"No. Not now. I'm no one's second choice."

The girls could not help it; they were dying laughing listening to the conversation between the two guys.

"I'm at the top of your list, right, Mike?" Jamie grabbed her hand as she tried to pass him en route to the chair on his left. Instead he pulled her down to sit on the couch between him and Josh. As her thigh brushed up against Josh's, an electric current sizzled through her.

She held her breath and looked up to see Josh's eyes upon her. There was nothing in his gaze that said he had felt it, too. This was ludicrous. She felt like such a fool. Of course he didn't feel the same electricity. She was his best friend. That was all.

She turned her attention back to Jamie. "Yes. You've always been my number one."

Micah leaned forward to grab her drink at the same time that Josh moved, causing them to bump arms.

"Sorry."

"Go ahead."

Micah wanted to go and hide somewhere. It was all so weird between them. Why couldn't she act normal around him? Why was she suddenly bumbling and clumsy in his presence? And she followed each with a round of awkward apologies. Surely everyone noticed the tension and weirdness happening so blatantly in front of them.

"Josh, what kind do you want?" Sabina held up two different types of beer for him to see.

"That one." He pointed to the one on the right. "And can you slice up one of those green lemons and stick it in the top?"

They all broke out in laughter, but Sabina rolled her eyes. It was a long-running joke with them. Seemed like forever ago, Sabina had made one of her silly comments about green lemons and no one had let her live it down since. *You mean limes, Sabina?* Josh couldn't help but be the one to point it out while the rest of them were snickering, leaving her clueless.

"Will you guys ever let that one go?"

"No." Josh came to get his own beer, because after that Sabina's generosity had run out. "You know I can't help teasing you about that one."

"Josh, one day you are going to say something stupid and I am going to have so much fun making fun of you."

"I seriously doubt that."

"No. I will."

"Oh, I'm sure you would, but I'm saying that I seriously doubt I will say anything that stupid."

"Oh, leave her be."

"What the—!" Josh bolted upright, causing the other four to turn their attention back to the television, and Lily giggled as he held her sideways under his arm like a football. Their team intercepted the ball and headed toward the red zone. All of them were on their feet, cheering the player on.

"Go! Go! Go!"

Then suddenly, ten yards from the end zone, the screen went black.

CHAPTER SIX

"I CAN'T BELIEVE your television broke!"

"Let's not talk about it." Josh massaged his temples, hoping to alleviate some of the building pressure.

He couldn't believe it. His freaking television had gone out right in the middle of the game. He'd missed the biggest play of the game because of that. He was still worked up over it.

He took his sports seriously. Most people from Boston did. You were asking for trouble if you came between a man and his sports, and that's exactly what his beloved big screen had done. What was he going to do about it?

Josh nursed his Red Brick brew, trying to not let it get to him. He would worry about it later. Micah, however, was a whole different situation. What was with the looks? It had taken everything in him to stay seated when she first walked in. The look she'd given him set him on fire, pushing every one of his self-imposed limitations to the brink.

"What's the score? I can't see it from here."

"I can't see, either, but I think we are winning still."

All five of them had ditched the apartment and sought out the nearest sports bar after Lily's mother came and picked her up. Loud, raucous patrons filled the space, but somehow they'd been lucky enough to find a table still within view of the television screens.

"You would know if we were losing. The whole bar would be yelling at the TVs."

"You're so right."

The waitress walked over to their table and set a fresh one down in front of him. He hadn't ordered it, nor was he finished with his first one.

"Thought you might want a refill," she said in a breathy voice.

Seriously? "Uh...thanks."

The waitress placed her hand on his shoulder. "No problem." She finally looked at the other occupants of the table. "Can I get anyone else anything?"

"I'd like a refill on my drink, please." Micah's snappy tone caused him to turn in her direction. She sat diagonally from him in the booth, for which he was grateful. If she were any closer, he would be coming up with lame excuses to touch her.

Micah gave the blonde waitress a once-over, clearly not liking what she saw. He had to stifle a laugh. The waitress returned with her refill and sent a big pageant grin his way before walking away again.

"Don't. Even. Think. About. It." Hanna poked him in the arm, accentuating each word. His four friends exchanged looks with each other.

"What?" He knew all about the impending lecture that he was about to endure, but feigned innocence, anyway.

"You know exactly what we are talking about." Jamie leaned back in the booth, both arms up and clasped behind his head. "You do it every time."

"Do what?" He couldn't stop the smile that broke out on his face.

"Lose the innocent act." Hanna jabbed an accusing finger in his direction.

"You know full well what you are guilty of, Joshua Taylor. We like this place and we won't let you ruin another one for us." They easily saw through Sabina. She didn't care about the place. She just hated when the attention wasn't focused on her. She preferred being the center of attention, and he loved messing with that. It had always been a source of contention between them, but neither of them would ever fess up to it.

"I do not ruin it for you." He took another long draw from his beer.

"Yes, you do!" Sabina sat forward in her seat.

"We like this place," Hanna pointed out.

"Well, other than that waitress." Josh's attention was immediately focused on Micah the moment the words slipped from her mouth. *She's jealous.* He could sense her irritation and had to bite back the grin that revealed way too much concerning just how that made him feel.

"You know…" Hanna said, bringing Josh back into the conversation. "If you go out with that waitress, it won't last. But her job here will and then we'll be forced to cross this place off our list, too."

He shook his head at the nonsense his four friends were spouting. They were too much.

"First of all, I'm not going to ask her out. And secondly, you guys act like this is a common occurrence. It's only happened a couple of times."

"A couple of times? Why are you suddenly being so modest?"

No one had ever accused him of being modest.

His friends all laughed in unison. So there was some truth to it. So what? He couldn't help the fact that wherever they went, bartenders, waitresses, hostesses would hit on him. On occasion he asked them out. What was the harm in that? He couldn't be blamed if they all turned out a little crazy.

"She's not even that cute." Jamie leaned back in his seat.

"Yeah, she's not worth it, Josh." Sabina said. "Fight the temptation and just say no."

"C'mon. Drop it already. I'm trying to watch a game here. I won't be asking her out. Rest assured. Your pub is safe."

"Yay! Thanks, Josh!"

They all laughed again.

After the game, Micah mentally kicked herself for leaving her stuff at Josh's apartment, including her car. When everyone else left from the pub, she was forced to head back to Josh's place. Alone. With him.

The tension in the air was palpable.

Well, to her it was. He was acting completely normal as he threw his keys on the counter and went in search of a trash bag from the kitchen.

Chips dropped by a three-year-old—and Jamie—still littered the floor near the couches. Half-empty drinks covered the coffee table. They had left in a hurry and hadn't bothered to clean any of it up.

She might as well help while she was here. It wouldn't be nice to just leave it for him to do alone. She sat her bag back down and grabbed a couple of empty cups and reached for the trash bag.

"You don't have to do this, Mike."

Why didn't it ever bother her when he called her that? She had snapped at Jamie for it earlier, and was constantly on Sabina's case about it, but every time the name slipped from his lips it sounded more like an endearment than a tease.

"I know, but let me."

"Fine. I'm not about to argue with you." In one swipe of his arm, he cleared everything off the coffee table and into the trash bag. "So we didn't get much of a chance to talk today."

That's because I've been avoiding you.

"How have you been? Has it been getting any easier?"

He meant the Drew issue, but she was more concerned with the issue at hand. Which had more to do with her fingers dying to trace the lines of the tattoo on his forearm. *Focus.*

"Yeah. It's been getting better. I have a plan in place and should have this whole thing settled in no time."

He stopped what he was doing, rising to his full six feet. His broad shoulders dominated the space, making him impossible to ignore. His dark eyebrow arched and the side of his mouth lifted in a half smile, the very same smile that left a good third of the women in Boston weak in the knees. Man, she was going to have to add her name to that list! "A plan?"

"Yes. I have it all worked out."

"Do you really think that's the best way to approach this?"

"Why not?" She shrugged her shoulders and got back to work.

"How does a plan help you control the dreams?"

She snapped to attention. "How do you know about the dreams?" She hadn't told him anything about them.

"Sabina."

A noise closely resembling a growl escaped from her before she could stop it. Sabina needed to mind her own business. Thank God she hadn't spilled everything about the dreams. How mortifying would that have been?

"She's worried about you, Mike."

"I really wish everyone would stop worrying about me. And talking about me. Mind your own business."

She carried the empty trays to the kitchen, and as she passed Josh, he jumped out of the way. Normally she wouldn't have thought anything of it. But since the other night, she'd found herself analyzing every move, every look, everything. And that quick leap to avoid touching her as she passed didn't need much dissecting. It wasn't a good sign. Not a good sign at all.

The slight drop in her shoulders couldn't be helped. Giving herself a mental shake, she made quick work of cleaning the serving trays.

He was scared to death. Like sweaty-palms, ragged-breaths and pounding-heart scared. Being alone with Micah left him terrified that he would once again do something to royally screw up their friendship. Things had taken a nosedive since the night he'd lost control and had her pinned underneath him on his bed.

She wasn't the same. The phone calls and text messages were decreasing and the space between them increasing. He couldn't make heads or tails of it.

And the way she kept looking at him—it was really throwing him for a loop. He was aware of the effect he had on women. He could see the signals long before they were even aware they were sending them. Micah had that look in her eye and he couldn't do a thing about it.

First, she was Drew's girl. Second, regardless of whatever plan she had in place, she was still in love with the guy and far from being over him. And third, she was his best friend, and that meant more to him than anything else in this world. Nothing was worth ruining that for.

He was a trained firefighter. He went head-to-head with death all the time. He could handle being in a room with her. It was just another fire he had to get under control. No big deal.

Just avoid touching her, brushing up against her, standing within two feet of her and looking at her.

Yeah, no big deal at all.

He had upset her when he brought up the dreams. He shouldn't have said anything. It really wasn't any of his business.

A week ago, they hadn't had any secrets between them. At least none that he knew about. She told him everything. It just further proved his point—that kiss had already done damage to their friendship, and he couldn't risk any more.

"Have you given the tattoo any more thought?" he called out as she placed the dirty dishes in the sink.

"Yes. How serious are you about that, anyway?"

"I'm always up for some new ink. What about you? Have you changed your mind?"

"Well, I've been thinking about it…"

"And?"

"I think I know what I want to get *if* I decide to do it."

Suddenly images of a tattoo on her flawless skin came to mind. Why exactly had he brought up this subject?

"Oh, okay. So *if* we do it, what are you going to get done?"

"Well, when I was going through those letters from Drew the other day I noticed something. He always signed his letter with a heart. Do you remember ever seeing it?"

"Me? No. He didn't sign his letters to me with hearts.

Or even write me letters. Now that I think about it, I'm kind of upset by that. I feel a little unloved."

"Ha. I'm sorry. I didn't mean to bring up a sore subject." She patted him on the knee. "Anyway...it was a unique heart. He did it in one stroke and looped the bottom where it came to a point."

"Okay, so you want to get this heart as a tattoo?"

"Yes. I want it to be something small that won't hurt me too much."

"Oh, don't be a baby about it."

She swatted at him, the palm of her hand hitting him in the middle of his chest. "I'm not. Plus, I want something that is personal to me and isn't so obvious to other people, like having his name engraved on my body."

Micah didn't move her hand. He looked down first at her hand, which rested over his racing heart, then up to find her eyes on him. How had he let her get so close?

Desire swept through his veins, forcing every cell in his body to zone in on the small, delicate hand that held him spellbound. She began to move it. He inhaled sharply and held his breath. Her hand made a torturous and slow glide from his chest and over his abdominal muscles as they contracted underneath her hot touch.

Slowly, she broke the moment as she pulled her hand back, formed a fist and rested it across her waist. He could hear her inhale as she took a deep breath. "So... when are we going to do this? Obviously, I'm free since I quit my job."

"Oh, that's right. How about later this week?"

"It's a date."

Stupid. Stupid. Stupid.

Micah was so mad at herself. For years she had lived

in blissful ignorance. Denial was a wonderful thing. Or it had been.

Now it was just bothersome and made her angry.

She had this plan in place, a set of rules to follow to finally put Drew's memory to rest. He was no longer allowed to dominate her mind. Which was all well and good, but somewhere along the way Drew went out and Josh came in.

And if she wasn't thinking about Josh, then she was thinking about Drew.

It was infuriating.

And Josh! Seriously?

They had been friends for twelve years now, and sure, there had always been an underlying attraction, but never something as crippling and all encompassing as it was of late.

Why did this have to come about now? Years ago would have been different. But now? It was an impossibility now. You couldn't go from being best friends for over a decade to this. It just didn't happen.

And the fact that she was even wasting time thinking about it now angered her the most. She would never, ever be capable of being the kind of woman he was attracted to.

Frustrating. Simply frustrating. But did that stop her? Nope.

At night she was tortured by thoughts of Drew, and during the day it was thoughts of Josh that threatened her sanity. She couldn't take any more.

For a girl who hadn't been on a serious date in years, she sure did have a lot of guy problems.

The night air was brisk; the sky was dark and gray. The unmistakable scent of fall surrounded her. Drew pulled her in close to his side as he whispered in her ear and charmed her with his sweet words. She turned to him, lifting her face to meet his lips in a kiss. Suddenly, he was gone and she was back in her room.

"Micah..."

She turned at the haunting sound of her mother's shaky voice. It caused her to sit up with a start in her bed, knowing immediately something was wrong. Her father was there, too, clad in a robe and slippers. They both sat down next to her on the bed, pulling her into their embrace. Her father's arms held her in a viselike grip, his breaths coming in quick succession. A feeling of trepidation coursed through her. Rapid thoughts of what could have happened raced through her mind.

"What? What happened? Is it Grandma?" *Her mother shook her head, telling her without words that it was not her grandmother. Tears fell from her mother's face.*

"Grandpa?"

"No, honey." *Her mother could barely get the words out.*

Her father was holding her so tight she could barely breathe, rocking her back and forth as her mother quietly sobbed next to her. Neither spoke for what seemed like forever. The silence was deafening.

"Baby, I'm so sorry. Drew..."

No!

"...Drew's gone to be with Jesus."

Micah's world collapsed. Her father held her tight as the gut-wrenching sobs took over. She felt robbed of air, robbed of thought. Robbed. It couldn't be real. This couldn't be happening. He was just with her. He had just kissed her good-night a couple hours ago.

It was all a lie! This was not happening! It couldn't be true. It was his birthday! People weren't supposed to

*die on their birthdays. Eighteen-year-olds weren't sup-
posed to die, period.*

No. No. No. No. No. This couldn't be real.

Micah jolted awake, sweat forming on her brow. She
reached for her teddy bear, drawing comfort from it as
the tears began to fall. Crying was her only way to release all of the emotions she still felt so vividly. No one
would ever understand it. Even she didn't understand
how after years without Drew, the pain could just return
with such vengeance.

Her mother had told her that grief was a unique emotion, that everyone's experience was different. Some
lasted longer than others. It was obvious the plan wasn't
working. Josh had been right. She had no way to control
the dreams, and as long as the dreams kept coming the
pain would never fully go away.

"Oh, Drew. Why do you keep doing this to me?"

She couldn't handle it anymore. She desperately
wanted to move on. It was only bringing up more pain
and it hurt too much. She was drowning here, drowning
in painful memories.

CHAPTER SEVEN

JOSH COULDN'T STOP thinking about the conversation he'd had with Jamie. Was he just coming up with excuses? He had always been aware that deep down he had feelings for her. But what was he supposed to do about that?

Nothing. That's what. He couldn't act on them. It wouldn't be right. He couldn't take advantage of their years of friendship—no matter what he felt.

He needed a distraction, something that would take his mind off of Micah for longer than an afternoon. He needed to get a date. And soon.

He walked toward the exit of the fire station, his shift over.

"Excuse me."

"Yeah?" Josh looked up to find a cute blond-haired woman standing next to the fire truck holding a cake. Distraction found. *Wow, that was quick!* "How can I help you?"

"The fire you guys put out yesterday was at my parents' house. I just wanted to thank you. Because of you guys, my parents are alive. I can't tell you how grateful I am." She came closer to him, batting her eyelashes. "Here. I baked a cake for the station."

"That wasn't necessary, but we'll take it, anyway. I, for one, have quite a sweet tooth." He looked down at the cake as she handed it to him. Chocolate, frosted with the worst attempt at "thank you" written across the top. The *u* looked strange, different from the rest of the word. He inspected it closer, trying not to appear rude, but it had him curious. She started to giggle. He looked up to find her blushing bright pink.

"I have to make a confession. I ran out of white frosting so I used toothpaste at the end."

"Oh." What the heck? Toothpaste? It both grossed him out and made him laugh. "And just what made you think toothpaste would be a good idea?"

"Well, I figured that way your sweet tooth would be both satisfied and cleaned. Win-win." A big white smile crossed her face. This girl was going to be fun.

"My name's Josh Taylor. I don't think I caught yours."

"That's funny. My name's Taylor, too." She flashed him a flirty grin that clearly showed she was interested. So was he. He would just have to talk to her about her multipurpose use of toothpaste.

"Well, come on in, Taylor. I'm sure the guys would love to meet you. And let's not tell them about the toothpaste. That will be our little secret."

He led the way into the firehouse to the common area. The guys were lounging on couches watching ESPN when they walked in the room. "Hey, guys. This is Taylor. She brought us a cake."

That caught everyone's attention. He couldn't be sure if it was Taylor, the cake or the combination that brought them all to attention with a chorus of "Hi, Taylor."

"We responded to the fire at her parents' house yesterday."

"Which one?"

"The one on Ninth."

"Oh. How are they doing?"

"Good. They lost a lot of things, but it can all be re-placed. We're just happy they are both safe."

"Do you have time for a piece of cake?" one of the guys asked her.

"No. I've got to get going. Thank you, though."

"Thank *you.*"

"I just came to drop off the cake and tell you how much my parents and I appreciate all you did."

"That was really sweet of you." Craig, one of the youngest at the station, began to approach her and Josh knew he had to step in.

"Here, I was on my way out, too. I'll walk you out."

"Thank you. That would be nice."

Josh guided her out of the room with a lightly placed hand on her back, staking his claim to the other guys. He glanced over his shoulder to see Craig stick his finger in the frosting, and the subsequent facial expression once he tasted the toothpaste mixed with fudge. *Yummy.*

"You didn't get a piece of cake."

He was hoping she had not noticed that.

"I'll text them to save me a piece. I'll be back later." A lie. He didn't want a piece of that cake. Not after knowing what she had used.

"Oh, good." When they made it to the front entrance, she stopped and turned to him. Her eyes dropped to the floor for a moment before turning them up to look at him. "I'm not usually this forward...but would you like to get coffee or something sometime?"

"Yeah. I'm up for that." They exchanged numbers quickly before she went her way and he went his. Man, he hoped this distraction worked. This was how he had handled it for the last decade. So why did he get the strong feeling it wouldn't work this time?

* * *

Taylor sat across from him in the cozy restaurant; a question resonated in her big blue eyes. Was she asking him a question? Shoot. What did she just say? She sat there, waiting for a response from him.

She tried again. "What are some things you like to do?"

She was so sweet and innocent. She had no idea he wasn't listening to her. He felt guilty. He *should* feel guilty. This was not how he typically acted on dates. It did not seem fair to her.

"I am usually up for anything on my off days. I hang out with my friends, play baseball in the summer…"

"That sounds like fun."

"Yeah. My friends are pretty great." Micah came to mind again. Dang, that girl could not leave him alone. "What about you?"

She was talking, and he did his best to pay attention. She deserved that much, although he wasn't starting out too well. He had already missed a good portion of her story.

"…when my brother died, it was one of the only things that made me feel safe again."

"I'm sorry about that… Your brother, that is." What was it that made her feel safe?

He really should be paying attention. But as he watched her lips move, his mind was invaded by thoughts of Micah's lips and how her bottom lip was slightly fuller than the top. And once that happened, his mind had to take a detour to remember every heated detail of their kiss. How her soft lips had responded to his. How her supple curves felt in his hands. How her body felt warm and willing beneath his.

Warm and willing? He was letting his imagination

run wild, apparently. He drained his glass of ice water and motioned for the waiter to bring more.

"There's just something about Neil Diamond's music that reminds me of those days when my brother was still alive and my family was whole. I feel at home again, safe and secure."

Hold the phone. She was talking about Neil Diamond?

"Do you know what I mean?" She looked at him over the rim of her glass of water. She took his silence to mean he needed further urging. "Do you have something or somewhere that makes you feel like you are safe with them?"

"Yeah. I do." *Micah.*

He was a jerk, a certified jerk for taking this girl out when his heart belonged to another. His heart had no business belonging to Micah, but that did not make it any less true. He needed to work harder to change that.

"Tell me more about your brother. What was he like? Older, younger...?"

"He was older, by five years. He was in the military. That's how he died, in the war. Before that he liked to do all kinds of things..."

She talked and he tried, but he just couldn't pay attention. Maybe she talked too much. Maybe it was the way she talked. Maybe he was developing adult-onset ADD. It was possible. He was sure of it. But no matter how hard he tried, he could not pay attention to what she was telling him. Instead he was noticing all the people in the restaurant: a group of friends laughing in the corner, a couple having a romantic dinner, another couple who appeared to be arguing and an older gentleman who sat by himself. All of them appeared more interesting than his distraction. Not much of a distraction at all. So much for that idea.

If he wasn't careful, he would end up just like the man sitting alone in a busy restaurant.

Josh needed a cup of coffee. His date with Taylor had been last night, and although the night had ended early for them, he had found himself walking around for hours afterward. There was a lot on his mind and it was all cluttering up his head.

He was on his way to work, a big shift ahead of him, so that cup of coffee was vital right now. He swung open the door to the coffeehouse he frequented near the fire station and stepped up to the counter. The girl behind the counter flushed bright pink as she took his order. The uniform had a tendency to do that, even when it was just the navy T-shirt with the fireman logo.

"It's on the house." He didn't think her face could get pinker, but it did.

Man, did he love the perks of his job. "Thanks."

Just as he turned to leave, a familiar flash of red caught his eye. Micah. She sat in the corner, near the window, completely immersed in a book. She did that when she read. She would get lost in the pages and be completely unaware of the world around her.

This was the Micah he was used to.

Her thick black frames sat perched on her nose as if they were sliding down and she had not realized it yet. Her hair was piled high in a messy knot on top of her head, a common look for her. She had let the girls talk her into bangs that cut straight above her eyes. He could tell they were bothering her and interfering with her concentration by the way she would blow them out of her eyes. The rebellious red fringe would float up for a moment, then settle back down onto her forehead.

He approached her slowly, not wanting to disturb her

yet. He enjoyed watching this side of her. As he got closer, he could see she was biting her lip. Her soft, full bottom lip enticingly trapped between her teeth. Torture. Pure torture.

As she turned the page, she switched to biting her thumbnail. The book must be a real nail-biter. He smirked at his own pun.

"So, is this another one of those books about the color gray?"

Her head snapped up. Big brown eyes stared back up at him from behind smudged lenses. "Hey. I didn't expect to see you here."

There was no smile, merely an acknowledgment of his presence. She usually greeted him with a big smile, one that made him melt.

"I work right around the corner." He indicated with his coffee cup.

"Ah. I guess I forgot about that. I'm here all the time, though, and I never see you."

"Maybe you're never looking. Too busy engrossed in your shady book."

"I am not reading *that* kind of book!"

"Just messing with you. What are you reading? Judging by your nails—" he lifted her hand to get a closer look "—it's pretty intense."

"A mystery."

"Makes sense."

She snatched his cup of coffee and took a sip. He would never allow anyone else to do something like that, but it was just one of her annoying traits—she was always curious what others were eating or drinking.

"Uck! What is that?"

He had to laugh at the grimace she produced.

"Are you gonna call that number?"

"What number?"

"The one written on your cup."

He lifted the paper cup and inspected it. There, above the logo, were digits hastily written in black Sharpie with a heart and the name Carrie. He looked over his shoulder to find the blushing girl leaning on the counter, staring in his direction. Upon realizing she had been caught, she quickly jumped up and got back to work.

"Um, maybe." He liked getting a rise from Micah. He wouldn't call her. He had no interest in blushing college students. They were a dime a dozen.

"Are you kidding me? She looks like she's barely out of high school."

"No, she doesn't. She's obviously older than that."

"Don't you have to get to work?"

"Yes, but I can take a few moments to hang out with my best friend. Don't you enjoy spending time with me?"

"Oh, sure, I love feeling like I'm at the center of an episode of *The Bachelor*."

He almost choked on his coffee as he laughed. "You know, sometimes you are really funny."

"I have an annual quota. That was my last one for the year. Hope you enjoyed it. Now go to work. I'm trying to read, and that girl is going to get fired if you don't stop distracting her."

"Okay, I'll let you get back to your book. See you later, Mike."

"See ya." With that she was back with her nose in the book. It was as if he had never even been there. He tried not to be offended by that as he headed to the door. He noticed the girl behind the counter again, still looking his way. He lifted his cup in her direction, acknowledging her, causing her to blush red again. It never got old.

* * *

Micah had set about her day purposely ignoring the dream she had the night before. A dream like that could easily set her back again.

Her mind wanted to get lost in the past again. Her heart craved the love she had once believed would last forever. But she couldn't do it. She wouldn't let herself go through this again.

Knowing her empty apartment was the last place she should be in this vulnerable state, she'd found refuge in a busy coffee shop and within the pages of a mystery novel. She'd never expected to see Josh, and with the current betrayal and instability of her heart and mind, he was the last person she wanted to see.

She didn't want to talk to him. Didn't even want to see him. His presence was a complication, and only made matters worse. How could she address one problem while he was creating new problems?

She'd kept the conversation light and casual and hoped her traitorous body wouldn't reveal anything about the effect he had on her. She had to stay away from him. For now, at least.

Micah had left the coffee shop shortly after Josh did, unable to focus on her novel any longer. She found herself back in her quiet and empty apartment. Sabina wouldn't be home until late, leaving her alone with her overpowering thoughts.

She tried to fight it, but the pull was intense. Her plan was an absolute failure. In an effort to neatly contain her grief in a box, she had only further remained lost in this grieving process. Healing would never happen until the grief was faced head-on, until she allowed herself to work through the emotions and to feel them one by one.

She was pissed. None of this was fair to her. She had

hopes and dreams, and long ago they had been centered around Drew. In an instant, everything had been stolen from her. She would never know what it would feel like to stand opposite him as he lifted her veil and claimed her as wife. She would never see the children they would have had. Would they have had Drew's bright blue eyes and her red hair?

She wanted to scream. She wanted to cry. She wanted to hit someone.

It wasn't fair!

She needed a distraction. Turning on some music, she cranked the volume and cleaned the apartment from top to bottom, hoping to redirect some of this hostility toward the grime building in the bathroom.

CHAPTER EIGHT

WORD HAD GOTTEN back to Micah that Josh had a new girl-friend. This new piece of information should not shock her or bother her. He was showing typical behavior. She was the one who had been acting abnormally lately.

He was allowed to date. She had no claim on him. Never had and never would. However, it did annoy her that he had started seeing someone and had failed to mention it to her the other day at the coffee shop. There had always been an unspoken understanding between them. She always met the girlfriends *before* they became his girlfriends. Her approval was required.

It shouldn't bother her, but *oh,* were her feathers ruf-fled. Hanna must have felt the same way, arranging a girlfriend meet and greet in the guise of a housewarm-ing party. Or maybe it was a housewarming party with the added bonus of being able to sneak a peek at the new girlfriend. It didn't matter.

She sat in her car, in Hanna and Nathan's driveway, seriously considering heading back home. She couldn't decide if she wanted to go in or not. Meeting the girl-friend was important, but she wasn't looking forward to seeing Josh again.

Micah turned the car back on and reached for her seat belt when a knock on the window made her jump.

Busted.

"Where are you going?" Jamie opened her car door and stuck his head inside. "If I have to be here, so do you."

"Oh, I just forgot—ah! Never mind." She let go of the seat belt, turned the car off again and bravely stepped out of the car.

"Dang, girl! You look hot!"

Heat rushed to the surface of her cheeks, and she was sure they were turning an embarrassing shade of red. She looked down at her black leather leggings and electric-blue suede booties.

She was trying something new in an effort to feel better about herself, but it had only caused her to second-guess herself more. She felt so insecure in the new clothes, but she kept recalling Sabina's lecture on confidence. *Confidence makes the outfit. You can pull off anything as long as you do it confidently.*

Therefore, she doubted her ability to pull off the look. "I don't look ridiculous?"

"Heck, no!" He grabbed her by the hand and pulled her along. "You're walking in with me."

"Wow. This place is crazy. I bet it cost a buttload of money." Hanna had been adamant about finishing the decorating before anyone saw it. It was impressive, to say the least. Colonial architecture provided history and elegance, but the modern upgrades gave it an element of luxury. "Hanna must be making a lot more money than she's been letting on. Next time we go out, we should make her buy."

"I was just thinking the same thing!"

The oversize front door opened to them as they walked up to it. Hanna greeted them, looking as if she'd just stepped out of a *Better Homes and Gardens* magazine with her happy-homeowner look. "Yay! You're here! Let me take your coats."

"Hanna, your home is gorgeous!"

"Thanks. Wow, Mike. Love the outfit."

"See? I told ya." Jamie's elbow shot out and nudged her in the side.

"Nathan, come get these coats and put them away," Hanna called out, disappearing into another room.

"Guess we have to give ourselves a tour."

"I think that sounds like a good idea." Taking Jamie's offered arm, she followed him as they went off to explore the huge house in all of its glory. Each room was filled with people—people in suits—Hanna and Nathan's type of people. Their conversations were even boring in passing.

She could hear Josh's voice coming from farther down the hall. A delicious tingle traveled down her spine. Never had the sound of his voice incited such a reaction from her. She told herself to get a grip. It was just Josh. BFF Josh.

It didn't matter what she wore or whether or not she wore it confidently. She would never turn his head. The girls he dated—and there were plenty of them—were of a higher caliber. They were girls who cared about their appearance, like, really cared. They had magnetic personalities. They tended to giggle at everything he said. He got attention everywhere he went.

He had never, not once, dated a bookish girl with glasses and an affinity for sweatpants. So it was absolute insanity to think he would actually look her way or think of her as anything other than a sister or best friend. Pure insanity.

Where was this coming from, anyway? Why the sudden resentment?

As she entered the room and caught sight of him, he automatically affected the temperature around her. He looked good. Really good. Drawn into the way his T-shirt hugged his muscled torso, she almost missed the girl holding onto his arm.

She was beautiful. Long blond hair hung in wavy curls around her shoulders. Her body was…well, it was dangerous. Maybe even lethal.

See? This was what she had to deal with. She needed to just forget about this and get some sense knocked into her.

Distracted by her wandering thoughts, Micah almost missed the introductions. She wasn't really paying attention. She caught the name.

Taylor.

Figured. She looked like a Taylor, all blonde and bubbly.

Was this jealousy? *What kind of a question is that? Of course it's jealousy!*

Micah forced a smile and waved her greeting to the new arm candy. She was being rude and she knew it. Josh would let her hear it later, but she couldn't help it. She just did not care right now. Why did she have to be nice to all of his interchangeable arm extensions?

He sent a perplexed look her way, which she chose to ignore. Let him think whatever he wanted. She wanted to leave, to go home. She was acting like a crazy chick with all her erratic roller-coaster emotions. There was no way she could handle being around him right now, especially with this Taylor girl at his side.

Micah left the room and ran into Hanna in the hallway. She reached out and grabbed her arm as she passed by. "I'm leaving, Han."

"What? You can't go!"

"I'm just not feeling good." She couldn't believe she'd just lied to her friend. What kind of person was she turning into?

"I don't care. This is a big night for me. This is my housewarming and engagement party." She let out a deep sigh. "Okay, I didn't mean that. I care if you really are sick. Are you really? Or is something else bothering you?"

"You're right. It's your big night. I'll hang out a little while longer."

"Thanks. If you really are sick, I'll forgive you if you have to go."

"Gee. Thanks."

If she could just steer clear of Josh and his new girlfriend then maybe, just maybe, she could survive this party.

"Come with me. I have someone I want to introduce you to."

Hanna took her by the wrist and pulled her into another room. She obviously didn't have a choice in the matter. "Just what I wanted tonight—a fix-up."

"He's really nice!"

"I'm sure he is."

Hanna pulled her to a stop in front of a very tall man in a suit. Yes, a suit. At a party.

Uh, I don't think so.

"Micah, this is Cameron Patterson. Cameron, this is Micah O'Shea."

"It's nice to finally meet you. I've heard so much about you." He stuck out his hand in greeting and she took it.

She glanced sideways at Hanna before speaking. "Oh, really? All good, I hope."

"Yes. Hanna has sung your praises."

"Has she now?" She threw another look Hanna's way. She would definitely kill her later. "So do you work with Hanna?"

"Yes. Are you a lawyer, too?"

"Me?" She laughed. "Oh, no. I'm…uh…in between jobs right now. Hanna and I have been friends for forever."

"Really? So you two grew up together?"

"Pretty much." Micah's eyes scanned the room without her realizing what she was doing—subconsciously looking for Josh. No sign of him.

Cameron wasn't bad on the eyes. He had to be at least six foot four, judging by how he towered over her. He had kind eyes and a pleasant voice, but none of it mattered. Her life was a mess, emotionally and physically.

She wanted to grab hold of his arms, look him in the eye and tell him, *You don't want me. I would be no good for you. I can promise you that.*

And that hurt.

Drew had ruined her by dying and leaving her to endure years of grief and pain, and by ruining all her best-laid plans and dreams.

Josh had ruined her, too, with the way he'd babied her all those years. Because of the attention he'd bestowed upon her and the affection he so easily gave, she'd never sought those things from anyone else. Therefore she'd never dated, never faced any of her issues, and most importantly, never healed.

She was of no use to anyone anymore. And it was all their fault.

Josh had no idea why he'd brought Taylor. She had called and asked what he was doing and on a whim he'd asked her if she wanted to come. But the moment Micah walked into the room, he knew he had made a huge mistake. What had he been thinking?

She'd strutted into the room wearing leather—*leather!*—leggings and high heels. Her black top dipped low in the front and he fought the urge to cover her with a coat. Her usually riotously curly hair, now straightened into submission, hung like silk around her shoulders and down her back.

Sabina and Jamie introduced themselves to Taylor, but Micah just gave a slight wave. He tried to read her eyes, tried to figure out what she was thinking, but failed.

She wasn't wearing her glasses tonight, having traded them in for contacts. He liked the unobstructed view of her eyes but missed the glasses. They were more like the Micah he was used to. He preferred her hair in a pony-tail and her nose buried in a book. He liked the sweat-pants. He was comfortable around that Micah. He could be himself around her. *Comfort* was not a word that could be used to describe what he was feeling now, with this new version of Micah standing before him.

Leather!

Their gazes locked, her poker-face expression still giving nothing away. She turned abruptly and left the room. The firm set of his shoulders relaxed as she walked away.

Every time she was near, his guard went up. It was becoming tiresome, always trying to protect. Protect himself from falling victim to his desires and ruining the best thing that had ever happened to him. Protect the promise he'd made to Drew to always take care of her, be the brother she'd never had, making her permanently off-limits. But even if he failed in all other areas, he would always work hard to protect Micah, even if that meant he had to keep her at a distance from himself.

He turned to find Taylor looking up at him. "You want something to drink?"

"You read my mind," she purred and gave him a co-quettish smile.

He headed toward the kitchen in search of refreshments, pushing his way past one too many suits. As he passed one doorway, she caught his eye. She was hard to miss. Micah stood off to the side, talking with a tall man in a suit. Her face was lit up with a smile as she laughed at something he said.

There was a huge part of him that wanted to storm into the room, knock the guy out, throw her over his shoulder and carry her away.

But the rational side told him to focus on getting the drinks he was sent to get. Micah was allowed to talk to men. She was allowed to laugh at their jokes. She was allowed to smile and flirt. She was allowed to do whatever she wanted.

But Mr. Tall Guy was *not* allowed to look down her shirt like he was doing.

Walk away. Just walk away.

Josh had to close his eyes and take a deep breath. And somehow he was able to walk away.

"Hey, Josh." He looked up to see an old friend approaching just as he made it to the drink station.

They talked for several minutes, catching up and re-hashing a few fond memories before promising to get together at some point. He spun around quickly to reach for a drink and collided with her.

Vibrant hair filled his vision. Soft, luscious curves brushed up against him. Her scent surrounded him, a mixture of a day at the beach and clean laundry—citrus and maybe coconut. It was the kind of scent that made him want to escape...with her.

"Sorry. That was clumsy of me. Did your drink spill?" He quickly apologized. She stood so close. Too close. His eyes took in her down-turned gaze, traveled past to the lip she was biting and even farther down to where her top dipped perilously low. His eager gaze took in the gentle swell of her breasts, the pale ivory expanse of divine skin...

You're such a jackass.

Inwardly he cringed. Five minutes ago he'd wanted to kill a man for doing the very same thing he had just caught himself doing.

"No. It was empty."

What was empty?

She avoided looking him in the eye, instead looking down at an empty cup.

Oh, the cup was empty. Made sense.

"Good." Why did this have to be so awkward? It had never been like this before. It had always been easy breezy. His eyes took in the leather leggings painted on her long legs and the bright blue heels that made them look even longer.

That's why. She had never dressed like this before.

She made a move to lean over again, brushing up against him as he did. "I just need to get to the soda. Can you hand it to me?"

The nerve in his neck twitched erratically as he clenched his jaw. She was going to be his undoing.

"Sure. Here you go," he choked out.

"Thanks."

"No problem."

She poured her drink and handed the two-liter bottle back to him before walking away, her hips swaying seductively.

"Hey, Josh? What happened to my drink?" He looked up to see Taylor's innocent face.

Good question.

CHAPTER NINE

MICAH GAZED AT the letter in her hands. Drew had given it to her on their two-year anniversary along with a solitary white rose. She lightly grazed her fingertips over the hastily written words—*I hope we're together for a long, long time.*

After leaving Hanna's house, she'd felt an overwhelming sense of...guilt? It didn't make any sense. Was it even possible to cheat on the ghost of a boyfriend past? Because that's exactly what she felt she'd done.

She couldn't get away from the new feelings she now had for Josh. The way she reacted to him, the type of thoughts she had about him.

Coming home to find the letter hadn't helped. After she had cleaned out the box of memories she had placed the letter on her dresser, not sure where else to put it now that she had done away with the box.

She felt she was becoming insane even to herself. She really should go see someone about this. It was all getting out of control.

Closing her eyes, she brought forth images of Drew. She tried to imagine what he would look like now. She imagined a beautiful house where they would have lived. A fireplace was lit where they sat in the living room, curled up on the couch. Drew's arm stretched across the back of cushions, beckoning her to curl up deeper into his embrace. She went willingly.

She looked up into his eyes, his cerulean gaze just as she remembered. His hair was shorter, cropped around his ears and neck. His clean-shaven jaw seemed sharper than before. She lifted her fingers to caress the hard, intense angles.

His kiss descended on her lips and she accepted lovingly with unveiled passion. Her hands wrapped around the back of his neck. Her fingers splayed out through his short hair, pulling him closer, needing more of him.

She gave herself completely to the kiss as it grew more and more heated. Without breaking the kiss, she moved to sit astride him, relishing the feeling of him underneath her.

His lips broke away from hers as he traveled down to the sensitive part of her neck. She threw her head back, desire taking over. She had never felt more alive. Her skin had never felt more sensitive, heightening every detail of his touch. Even the way the coarse stubble on his face scratched against her skin excited her.

Her eyes flew open, her body frozen as she recalled the smooth angles of Drew's skin.

His head lifted; their gazes locked.

Not blue.

Gray.

Her vision was clouded by the desire he ignited within her, but she couldn't mistake the heat in those steel-gray eyes.

Josh.

It wasn't supposed to be him! She needed to get off of him. She needed to breathe. But just as she tried to move, he pulled her back down hard against him.

He wanted her. And if she finally faced the truth, she wanted him, too.

The nip at her neck was her breaking point. Her resolve wasn't just weakened, it was destroyed. She felt herself melt into his embrace.

Micah framed his face with both hands, wanting to look him in the eyes, to know whom she was kissing this time. His lips met hers in a demanding kiss. His tongue, sliding between her lips, entangled with her own.

She had never known such desperation, such need.

Josh pushed her back onto the couch, moving with her. He deepened the kiss as he positioned himself on top of her. Instinct drove her to wrap her legs around him, tightening the connection until space no longer existed between them.

One hand remained entwined in his hair while the other drifted down his back. The muscles rippled underneath the cotton of his T-shirt as her fingers grazed down his spine. Her hand slipped beneath the cotton to touch the heated skin of his torso. Her greedy fingers roamed to his front and moved slowly, tortuously over him. The animal-like sound he emitted further ignited her arousal.

Alarms went off in Micah's head, but she ignored them. Instead she grabbed hold of the shirt and yanked it up. She needed it gone. Now. He obliged, pulling away from her only long enough to take it off.

The shock of feeling skin on skin forced her to look down. In the midst of her desire, she was unaware that he had unbuttoned her top and pushed it aside.

The alarm sounded again, piercing through the fog. She couldn't stop even if she wanted to.

His large masculine hands moved over her—

"Micah!"

She bolted upright at the sound of Sabina's shrill voice.

"Turn that stupid alarm clock off and get up! You've got your interview in an hour!" Sabina yelled from the other room.

Micah's gaze took in the sheets tangled around her ankles, her comforter discarded on the floor beside her bed.

She put a hand to her chest, feeling the rapid beating of her heart. That was some dream!

"Micah!"

"I hear you! Jeez! I'm up."

Micah jumped in the shower before Sabina could get a look at her. She knew one look would be enough for Sabina. She would know something was up and then be on her case, demanding details.

The cold water was a shock to her still feverish skin. Goose bumps puckered on her flesh as she forced herself to withstand the punishment for just a moment longer before turning the dial in the opposite direction.

She showered quickly and readied herself for the interview. She needed to focus if she had any hope of making it through this day. And she really needed this interview to go smoothly.

Donning the navy suit Hanna had let her borrow, she studied her reflection in the mirror. For some strange reason she expected to see it written on her face for the world to see that she had had another steamy dream about Josh last night. She was shocked when she didn't see it staring back at her in the mirror. Though her cheeks were still a vibrant shade of pink. It looked good on her.

"My, my. Don't you look nice." Sabina gave her a once-over when she entered the kitchen to grab a cup of coffee.

"I try."

"Did you have a rough night last night? Your alarm

clock was going off for twenty minutes this morning. Drove me crazy."

Heat filled her cheeks. "Sorry."

Sabina's eyes widened before a slow smile formed on her face. She looked like a cat who ate the canary. "You had another steamy dreamy!"

"Oh, my gosh. We are *not* talking about this."

"Oh, yes, we are. Sit back down. I need details. Who was it about this time? Ooh, ooh! That tall drink of water that Hanna introduced you to!"

"No. And FYI, no one says *tall drink of water* anymore."

Sabina waved a dismissive hand. "He was tall and hot. Who cares what you call him, just make sure you, you know, call him."

Micah stirred some creamer into her coffee and took a tentative sip, not wanting to burn her tongue.

"So who was it? Did you meet someone else last night?"

"No. And I'm not telling you a thing. Last time I told you about a dream, you went and blabbed about it. Can't trust you with anything."

"Wow, that was harsh."

"I've got to go. Can't be late for the interview."

"I'll wear you down. You'll break eventually. Mark my words."

Micah ignored her and reached for her purse.

"Good luck, bestie!"

Her interview was a success. Of course, there was the standard waiting period before they would call and offer the job, but she was almost positive they would.

She felt as if she was floating as she walked out of the building and onto the busy streets of Boston. With her current cheery mood, going home sounded like the worst idea ever, so she made an impulsive decision.

It was scary going alone, but in spite of the fear and lack of best friend, she found herself in a parlor chair in the corner of a cramped tattoo shop. This was something she needed to do on her own, anyway. It symbolized the next phase in her life, and that required more independence.

The pristine navy suit she wore stuck out like a sore thumb in the little shop, and she was getting a few odd looks from the random patron or artist.

A man stood and called her name. It was time. She shucked the suit jacket and sat down in the chair, telling him exactly what she wanted.

The tattoo artist leaned heavily on her as he concentrated on getting the template in the right place. The room had a vague antiseptic scent mixed with cigarettes. The smell had a negative effect on her, causing her stomach to churn.

When he started tattooing the ink on her skin, she closed her eyes and focused on the music playing overhead and the hum of the machine next to her. She knew it would hurt, but she wanted this. Once she made up her mind, nothing was going to stop her, even if she had to do it alone. So she chose the small heart design and ignored the pain.

"We get a lot of requests for hearts," the artist said as he concentrated on getting the thin lines just right. "But this is the first one I've done like this. It's kind of different. I like it. Does it have a special meaning to you?"

"Yes. It does." She didn't want to explain it, so she kept it at that. He seemed to accept it as a sufficient answer, because he just nodded and kept working. It didn't take long at all. She was surprised at how quick he was.

Micah peered over her shoulder into the mirror to see her fresh ink. There on her left shoulder was the tiny heart that she had chosen. Looking at its dainty lines, she knew she had made the right choice. At least this way part of his heart would always be with her.

It was perfect.

Taylor must have sensed that he wasn't as into her as she was into him. After he'd handed her her drink at Hanna's party, she'd walked away and he barely saw her the rest of the night. At one point, he saw her talking to a group of guys. Later, she left with one of them.

His ego was bruised for sure. He had never had a date leave with someone else. Not ever. He must be losing his touch. At least it saved him from having to end it with her. He didn't feel right leading her on, anyway. Now that he had finally come to grips with how he felt about Micah, he couldn't stomach the thought of being with anyone else.

His future looked bleak. Micah would never truly be his. And if he couldn't date anyone else, he was headed for a long and lonely life.

He was pathetic.

He woke early and went for a run. Running always gave him clarity of mind to help him sort things out. It also released all his tension and eased his frustration. And to be honest, he was fraught with tension and frustration these days. With that in mind, he doubled up his normal route and picked up speed, pounding it all out on the pavement.

CHAPTER TEN

MICAH HAD NOT dressed up for Halloween in years. It was a child's holiday. Grown-ups passed out the candy. They did not participate. However, in going along with her newly adopted theme of making changes in her life, she succumbed to another one of Sabina's wonderful ideas and dressed up as a butterfly for a Halloween party at Sabina's new boy toy's place.

Her costume was far from what she would have picked out, but Sabina always had a way of making her do or wear something she would regret later. *Note to self...stop doing everything Sabina tells you to do and learn to say no.* Micah had no idea that butterflies had a skanky species, but here she was clad in a miniskirt and tights, with glittery wings and rainbow eyelashes.

Since the party was being held at Sabina's boyfriend's place, she had left without Micah in order to help out with some of the hosting duties. Funny, she never helped with any of those duties when they hosted a party.

Micah exited the apartment building, holding her wings in her hand, and pulled her jacket tighter around her. It had been snowing pretty badly, but she was Massachusetts born and bred. She could handle anything.

Deciding she needed a cup of coffee, she forced her way through the heavy snow toward her favorite coffee drive-through only to find it closed. *Hmm…* She parked her car and trudged through the snow. It had to be open. Maybe their drive-through was just closed. But as she reached for the door, she came face to face with a large orange-and-black closed sign crushing her hopes.

Great. Just great. What in the world were they closed for? It was Halloween, not Christmas.

She turned back toward the parking lot and just then noticed it was empty. She should have seen that before getting out in this weather. She turned on the car and waited for it to heat up again, flipping on the music and singing along. Putting the gear in reverse, she turned to see behind her, but was surrounded by a blanket of white. She pressed on the gas, but nothing happened. She tried again. Still nothing. *Seriously?*

Micah was stuck. She was stuck in the snow. Stuck in an empty parking lot with no one around to help. While dressed like a skanky butterfly. *Just great.*

She put the car back in park and pulled her phone out. Immediately she went to Josh's number, but stopped just before hitting the green button. Instead she pulled up Sabina's number. It rang, but no answer. That girl never answered her phone! She tried Hanna, but when it went straight to voice mail she remembered the big meeting she'd said she had tonight. Jamie was too far away. That just left Josh.

She called, and just like she expected, he answered and was on his way.

Why did he always have to play the role of her hero, her knight in shining armor? She would never learn how to make it on her own if she was constantly depending on him to run to her rescue.

Sure, focus on your newly found need for indepen-

*dence. Ignore the way your whole body is teeming with
longing at the thought of seeing Josh.*

As images of her dream the other night invaded her
mind, she was forced to remove her scarf and undo the
buttons of her heavy coat. She was so hot she could turn
the car's heater off and stay warm for days just thinking
about that dream.

Trouble up ahead.

Deep, deep trouble.

She called, he came running. It was as simple as that. It
didn't matter that warnings about the impending snowstorm were blasting on every television and radio station.
In fact, it only made him move faster.

What he did not understand was why in the world was
she out in this mess in the first place. Hadn't she listened
to the news? Forget that. Hadn't she noticed the blanket
of white that covered everything in sight? Even his big,
heavy truck was sliding on the slushy streets. Her car
would never survive in this.

In the distance he could barely make out her white
Camry, already blending into the snowy backdrop. He
plowed through the snow building up in the small coffee
shop parking lot and pulled up next to her. She hopped
out of her car and quickly jumped into his truck.

Her hood fell back as she settled into the seat, revealing part of a Halloween costume. Crazy-colored false
eyelashes fluttered erratically as she buckled her seat
belt. He shook his head.

"You were going to a Halloween party in this? Are
you kidding me? Are you insane?"

"There's no need to be rude. I understand *now* how
foolish an idea it was."

"You think?" He carefully steered back onto the road,

trying to catch a few peeks at her costume without losing control of the truck. "What are you supposed to be? Tinker Bell?"

"No. I'm a butterfly."

"A butterfly? This just keeps getting better. What happened?"

"I was headed to the party and stopped for a coffee. I thought the road conditions were doable."

"Well, Tink, your car should be fine here overnight. Hopefully we can get it out tomorrow. We might have to dig it out, though."

"Butterfly, you moron!"

He kept his eyes on the road, fully aware that the conditions had drastically worsened since he had first left his apartment. It was almost impossible to see the lanes, and even if he could, he wouldn't be able to stay in them. His truck felt like a puck on an air-hockey table, gliding back and forth. "Listen. These streets are getting really bad. I can take you back to your place, but then I'd be stuck there until it clears up. Or I can bring you back to my place, where you would be stuck."

"My place is closer."

The ride to her apartment was silent and awkward, at least on his side of the truck. This didn't happen often for him. He liked to be in control of the conversation. If people weren't comfortable and laughing around him, it just felt weird. He always felt responsible for breaking the ice and easing the awkwardness, but this time he was the awkward one. No amount of jokes or casual banter could dispel the tension making itself at home in his truck.

Pulling up to the Victorian where she lived, he finally let out the breath he had been holding. They'd arrived in one piece, but barely. There was no way he would make it home in this. He shook his head, thinking about how dumb it was that Micah had actually thought she could make it to a party tonight. She ran inside while he made sure his truck was all sealed up. There was nothing worse than realizing you had left a window or a door cracked in a snowstorm. His truck was his baby. He was not letting anything happen to her.

After lifting the wiper blades off the windshield, he headed into Micah's building. It was going to be a long night. Thank God Sabina would be around. For once he was grateful for their combative relationship. It would take his mind off of things.

He climbed the stairs to her apartment. Her front door was ajar, her snow-covered shoes appearing to have been shed midstep, blocking the doorway. He kicked them aside and placed his next to them, careful not to step in the quickly growing puddle of melted snow.

It was quiet—too quiet. "Where's Sabina?"

"She's at the party already."

Of course she is.

"You should have seen *her* costume. She is going to be miserable in it all night."

"Oh, I can only imagine what she would have worn."

She yanked off her jacket and threw it on the chair by the door. Something caught his eye. Her shoulders were bare, revealing portions of her back. If he was not mistaken, he could have sworn he saw a tattoo on her shoulder. Had she gone without him? Work had caused him to cancel on her, but he'd just thought she would postpone and wait for him.

As she walked from the living room to the kitchen and then disappeared into her bedroom, he strained to make out what the tiny new piece of ink was. It was a heart, but it wasn't the one she'd said she was going to get. No, this heart was different. Why had she changed her mind?

She had left him alone in the apartment. This was awkward. It never had been before, but it definitely was now. After twelve years of friendship, things suddenly felt alien between them. He didn't know what to say or what to do. He definitely didn't feel comfortable touching her anymore. The easiness that had once been a natural part of their relationship now ceased to exist. "I'm going to use your bathroom."

"Yeah, go ahead."

When he returned, she still had not come out of her room. "Mind if I make myself some coffee?"

"You know where everything is?" she yelled back through the door.

"Yup." Not that it was difficult. She had one of those cheat machines: insert prepackaged coffee cup into machine and hit the button. Ready in under a minute. No one could ruin that. "You want a cup?"

"Yeah. I never made it into the coffee shop. They were closed."

"Even the coffee shop had the good sense to stay home tonight," he mumbled under his breath.

"I heard that," she said, surprising him from behind.

"Which kind do you want?"

"Hazelnut, please." She had changed into sweatpants, her typical Micah wear. Her makeup had been washed off, contacts removed and the familiar black-framed glasses were back in place. He could handle this; butterfly wings and leather leggings, not so much.

"Did you have dinner yet?"

"No." His stomach took that moment to grumble, as if in response to her question. She heard and laughed. "Guess I'm hungrier than I thought."

"I'll throw something together then. Let's see what I've got here...hmm. Sabina has provided us with so

many healthy options. Yuck. Stir-fry doesn't sound too
bad. What do you think?"

"That's fine with me."

"Here, slice these up." She handed him zucchini, carrot and onion. "Cutting board's under there."

He stared at the vegetables in front of him, trying to
figure out how to go about this task.

"So how's Taylor?"

"Who?" Josh looked down at the onion. "You know I
hate cutting onions. I hate them, period."

"Oh, get over it. Stop being such a baby." She spun
to get something else out of the fridge. "And what do
you mean, *who?* Taylor. Your girlfriend. Is that not her
name?"

"Oh. Yeah." He had forgotten about her. How could
he not when he was in Micah's presence?

"Did you forget you had a girlfriend?"

"No. She's not my girlfriend. We just went out once or
twice. I haven't even really seen her since Hanna's party."

"Oh."

Why did he just tell her that? He could have used Taylor as a buffer without Micah being any wiser.

He could not help but try to gauge her response, watching for any sign or hint as to how Taylor's presence in his
life affected her. She gave up nothing. This was ridiculous. They had been friends forever. He could not think
of a person he trusted more. And what he was thinking
about, what plagued him day and night, could easily ruin
it all. It was not worth it.

"You want beef or chicken?"

She stood by the open refrigerator waiting for his response. But he could not think around her anymore.

"Josh? Are you all right? You seem off tonight."

He shook his head, trying to clear his mind. "Sorry. Beef." This was going to be a long, long night.

"I didn't really get a chance to talk to her the other night. What's she like? Tell me about her..."

"She's great. She, uh...likes Neil Diamond and stuff."

"Mmm...she sounds very interesting. Where did you guys meet?"

"The firehouse."

"She works with you?"

"No." What was with the twenty questions? He didn't want to answer questions about Taylor. Mainly because he did not know the answers. And talking to Micah about other girls was just strange.

"No?"

She would not stop until he answered her questions and her curiosity was satisfied.

"We put out a fire at her parents' house two weeks ago."

"That's nice."

"Yeah, you know, we've had fun together so far."

"What? Singing 'Sweet Caroline'?"

"No, we talk and hang out."

"Already this is sounding better than Miss Just-Changing-the-Lightbulb."

"Actually, she turned out to be *Mrs.* Just-Changing-the-Lightbulb."

"She was married? And needed help changing a lightbulb?" She tossed him a judgmental glance over her shoulder, shaking her head. "You sure know how to pick them. But let me guess, this one is different, right?"

"Well, so far this girl knows how to change a lightbulb *and* knows how to get herself home in a snowstorm."

"Ouch!" He loved the way her face lit up when she laughed. "Good one."

"I try."

He chopped and diced the vegetables as instructed while she started cooking. When he was finished with his given tasks, he leaned against the counter and held his coffee in one hand. Micah turned and gave him a quick once-over, laughter filling her eyes.

"What?"

"Your zipper is down."

He looked down and sure enough, it was. He looked back up at her as she giggled. "It's been down this whole time and you're just now telling me? My eyes are up here, Micah. Let's try and keep yours above my waist level."

"Ha! Whatever! I was *not* checking you out." Micah swatted at him with her spatula, but he was quick enough to duck out of its path. She countered with her other hand and there was no hope of escaping that one.

"You totally were, and you know it." This was easier. More like how it used to be between them. He zipped up his pants and went back to his coffee.

They cooked in comfortable silence—at least, that was what it was supposed to be. Josh remained on edge, though. Each time she came close or accidentally brushed up against him, he tensed. He prayed she would not notice. He kept throwing out his typical jokes to keep her off his trail. If she caught on or noticed, she showed no sign or it.

"How is it coming?" She stretched to look over his shoulder to see his progress with the dinner. He had a lot of practice cooking for the guys at the firehouse and was pretty good at it. She was impressed. He might even be better than she was with all the slicing and dicing.

"I'm almost finished with all the veggies. The meat looks like it's just about ready for the rest of the stuff."

"You are right. It does look like it's ready." Micah armed herself with a spatula and got back to work.

Josh was acting a little weird. He was trying to cover it up, trying to act like normal, but she knew him better than that. Could he tell? Was she that easy to read?

She did want to be independent from him, to be able to function without needing him in every area of her life, but she didn't want to lose his friendship altogether.

As she worried about the state of their relationship, she mindlessly stirred the ingredients in the hot pan on the stove top. "Can you pass me that jar of minced garlic?"

"Sure."

He handed it to her and she scooped out some to add to the pan. With the open jar of garlic in one hand and the lid in the other, she quickly turned to return it to the fridge, attempting to close it midturn. When she whipped around in the small kitchen, she collided with Josh as he also tried to get to the fridge. The minced garlic in olive oil went all over his shirt as the jar dropped to the ground, shattering and covering the floor.

"Oh. My. Gosh." She shook her hand, trying to rid herself of the garlic clinging to her hand. It only made things worse, sending it flying in the air. "I am so sorry!"

They both lost it, laughing until they cried. It reeked around them, the smell of garlic filling the air. They began to pick up the large pieces of glass and made quick work of cleaning up the stinky mess. She washed her hands, knowing full well they would smell for days. Looking up at Josh for the first time since the incident, she was reminded of the mess she had made of his shirt.

"I've ruined your shirt!"

"It will be fine, I—"

"No. It's not fine. You'll never get the oil out. And the smell… Girls will stop talking to you altogether."

"Maybe I want the girls to stop, anyway."

"Yeah, right. I think I have one of your old Red Sox T-shirts…"

His eyebrow formed a perfect questioning arch.

"I stole it from you years ago. Get over it."

She went in search of the T-shirt, digging through her drawers. Hopefully it wasn't dirty. She liked sleeping in it. Thankfully, she found it clean and folded in a drawer.

She turned to head back to the kitchen only to find he had followed her into her room. He stood there just inside her doorway, ruined T-shirt in hand, chest bare.

Wow, did he fill up the place! She could not control her eyes from feasting on the expanse of tattooed skin.

She had been there when he had two of the tattoos done, but she did not remember reacting like this. Her fingers itched to trace the ink, especially the intricate design that covered the whole left side of his torso. And what a torso it was. She remembered the pain he had endured during that tattoo session, his grip tightening during moments of intense pain as she held his hand the entire time.

"Can I have the shirt or not?"

Oh, my gosh! She was still holding the T-shirt in her hand while staring at him like a desperate and starved woman. Quickly, she dropped her eyes to the floor, very much interested in the wood floors and their need of a good sweep.

She still hadn't relinquished the shirt. This was getting embarrassing. She tossed it at him, but he still blocked the doorway. She was stuck, forced to watch him clothe himself.

What a shame to have to cover it all up, but if she wanted to keep her sanity it needed to happen.

Boy, was it hot in here! What was the thermostat on,

anyway? His eyes connected with hers once more before he turned to leave the room.

"Thanks. You know what this means, though."

"What?" She felt anxious, wondering what in the world would come from his mouth next. Had he noticed the way she had looked at him? What was he thinking? Her heart raced as she waited for his response.

"I'm taking my shirt back."

She exhaled deeply. Giving up the shirt was easy enough; an awkward conversation about her gawking at him...not so much.

CHAPTER ELEVEN

JOSH KNEW.

This was it. She was done for. She had been blatantly obvious in the way she stood there like a sex-starved crazy person when he took off his shirt earlier. How could she be so stupid?

He was acting even worse now than before. Of course, he was still trying hard to cover it up, acting so close to normal that a person watching them interact would not know something was up.

But she did.

Micah put on a movie, waiting for him to nix her choice, but he didn't. Yup, something was up with him.

He sat at the opposite end of the couch, the farthest point away from her. He kept his focus on his plate, as if he was afraid the food would jump off or something. He was trying so hard to act normal, but it was just coming across all wrong. He didn't want to be there with her. He didn't want to show it, but she could see the truth.

She missed her friend. She missed how things used to be before Drew's anniversary, before she screwed it up by getting drunk and kissing him. She had made things awkward between them. He didn't like her like that, and didn't know how to tell her.

Micah had hoped the funny movie would lighten

things up, but half an hour into it he still hadn't laughed or even broken a smile during any of the hilarious scenes.

If she had any hope of making it right between them, now was her chance. She had to decide now to either take a giant risk and explore these new emotions *or* she needed to lock them away forever and never look back.

As she chewed on her nails, contemplating this monstrous and high-stress decision, Josh lifted the remote and hit the stop button.

Her head snapped to attention. "What did you do that for?"

"You weren't watching it."

"Was, too."

"Oh, stop. You weren't and you know it. You were biting your nails and thinking about something. I can tell when something is bothering you, you know. Let's talk."

She gulped. "Okay..."

"What's bothering you?"

"Nothing's bothering me. I don't know why you keep saying that. What's bothering you?"

"You seriously aren't going to talk to me about it?"

"How can I talk to you about it if I don't even know what you are talking about?"

"Is it about Drew? You haven't brought him up lately. Are you still having dreams about him?"

She was having difficulty swallowing around her heart lodged in her throat, the rhythmic beat of it pounding in her ears. If he only knew just what she had been dreaming about these days.

Drew still plagued her, but not as much as Josh now did. She was a work in progress, slowly working through her issues and taking it day by day. But she didn't want to talk about Drew.

She wanted to touch him so bad it hurt. She had to go

for it. There was so much to lose, but if she was going to go mad and ruin things regardless, she might at least give it a shot before that happened.

"Fine. I'll talk." Micah turned to face him, leaning back against the arm of the couch and extending her legs until her bare feet reached him. Her sweatpants had ridden up her legs as she slid them in his direction, exposing goose bumps that had nothing to do with the cold. She wiggled her toes against his solid thigh. She took a deep, stabilizing breath. "My feet are cold, though. Will you hand me that blanket?"

Okay, so she wasn't very good at playing the role of seductress.

"Where are your socks? You've got goose bumps, crazy girl." He took hold of her feet and lifted them onto his lap, rubbing them briskly in an effort to warm them.

This was so silly. She felt ridiculous!

He grabbed a blanket from the basket next to the couch and draped it over her legs, carefully tucking it around her feet.

A caring and brotherly move.

Argh!

This was an epic fail.

"Do you think we'll be friends forever, or do you ever wonder if we're heading in different directions?" Why had she asked that? She just needed to give up now. "I mean, like the group of us. Sometimes I wonder how long this will last with all of us still being friends. I want it to last, but I wonder if it will. We all seem to want such different things in life."

She was just rambling now. Nothing that came out of her mouth made any sense.

"Just because we all want something different or are maybe heading in different directions doesn't mean we can't still be there for each other. I know that you've been struggling lately with Drew's anniversary. And I know that it seems like none of us care anymore. It probably worries you that he was the only thing that held us all together, and if we move on from him then we all fall apart. But I don't think that will happen. He may have brought us all together, but he isn't what holds us together."

"I guess you're right."

"I think it's the same with any relationship. You've got to make the conscious decision that no matter where you are in life, you make time for the ones who matter most. You put in the effort and make it work."

But what about us? "Will you always make time for me, Josh?"

"I'm not going anywhere."

"You promise?"

"Actually, I was contemplating a best friend upgrade, but since you're getting all serious on me, I'll pass and let you stick around."

"Gee, thanks. Always knew I could count on you."

"But seriously…" He grabbed her ankles and pulled her close to him so that her legs draped over his lap. He wrapped his arm around her and held her close. "I'll always be here for you. No matter what."

Temptress she was not. Best friend forever was the more appropriate title.

The moment he pulled her onto his lap he knew he had made a huge mistake. Her legs were draped over his lap, her head on his chest. He had one arm wrapped around her while the other was inching closer to dangerous territory. He let his hand relax as it hung over her upper thigh, but if he moved it a centimeter he would be touching her.

It would be too easy to drag his hand up, to explore the forbidden peaks and valleys of her beautiful form.

Amid the comfort of her in his arms, his body and mind battled it out. He wanted to pull her against him, kiss her senseless, show her all that had been culminating within him. But he knew it was wrong. He knew he should push her back to her side of the couch, a safe distance between them.

He pressed play on the remote and the movie started where they had left off. Against his better judgment—which was how he did things these days, apparently—he draped the blanket over the both of them to fight off the chill of the long, cold, wintry night they had ahead of them. They remained nestled on the couch, neither of them moving from their positions, warm and snuggled together. The fierce wind blew hard and hail pinged against the windowpane, but he wasn't paying any attention.

"Sorry for being so difficult lately." She spoke quietly against his chest. He could almost feel her words more than he could hear them, the vibration moving through his chest. She lifted her face to look at him, her eyes bright and full of an emotion he couldn't distinguish. She'd always been like that: felt too hard, loved too much.

"What are you talking about?"

"The last couple of months. You know, first with the depression. I was so needy. Then with the... Well, anyway. I've just been a pain. Maybe I've been that way for years.... I don't know how you've put up with me for so long."

"You haven't been that bad."

What she was going through was normal and could be justified. He, however, had no excuse for his behavior.

"You're a liar, but thank you. I'm hoping this is the end of it, though. I think I'm finally ready to move on."

"And are you? Moving on?"

"Sometimes I feel like I have moved on. Then other days, it seems difficult to let go. Two steps forward, one step back. And every time I feel this sense of guilt for even trying to move forward."

"I know what you mean." He knew exactly what she meant.

"You do?"

"Yes. It feels like you're dishonoring him and his memory."

"Exactly." Her response was a whisper on his neck.

She leaned into him, her face buried in his neck. Her lips innocently came in contact with the skin just below his ear. Electricity coursed through him as his hold on her tightened. He closed his eyes, praying sanity would return.

Focus on the subject at hand. Something platonic. Focus on Drew. Or your mother!

That worked.

He thought about the important things. Micah considered him to be her safety and he took the job seriously. He would make sure she always felt secure with him. The images that ran through his mind threatened that in every way possible. He'd begun to recite it to himself, a mantra of sorts: *Drew's girl. Drew's girl.*

"I think I've always felt guilty for living, guilty for turning him away that night, for ignoring my instincts and letting him drive in that storm. I didn't feel like I deserved to live life, much less a happy life."

Her words hit too close to home. His own guilt was overwhelming. He could take hers away in an instant, but he would lose her just as fast. She would hate him if she knew the truth. She would never forgive him. "You have nothing to feel guilty about. It was just his time to go."

"Yeah. I think I've finally figured that out. And that we honor his memory best by living a life he would be proud of. You know he always lived life to the fullest. He would expect the same from me."

They watched the rest of the movie in silence, but his mind was far from quiet. He kept thinking about what she had said about Drew wanting them to live life to the fullest. Part of him wanted to believe Drew would have supported anything that made Micah happy. But what if he couldn't make her happy?

He had never wanted anything more from a woman than a casual relationship. He'd never allowed anything deeper to happen between him and someone else. What if he wasn't capable of a long-term commitment? What if he hurt her? Josh didn't want to believe that he would ever intentionally do that to Micah, but why risk it?

None of it mattered, anyway. He was wasting brain-power just thinking about it. At the end of the day, Josh knew the truth about Drew's wishes. Nothing could ever, ever happen between him and Micah. The end.

The movie credits began to roll, but Josh couldn't move. He didn't want to. Micah's deep and steady breathing told him she had fallen asleep on his chest. She felt so right. He wanted to hold his breath so as not to disturb her. It felt natural to have her there, fitting so well next to him. It was as if he had been made just to hold her like this.

His emotions were running ragged. Recently, there had been times he felt so angry at her, at this situation and her inability to move on from Drew. But he loved her deeply and the moment she looked up at him with her warm coffee-colored eyes, his anger dissipated.

But more often than not, there were moments, moments he was ashamed of, moments of pure lust that should never have happened. She didn't belong to him. She never would.

Sitting here any longer would be detrimental to his state of mind. He really should carry her to her bedroom and leave her there, safely ensconced behind a locked door.

But instead he found himself carefully readjusting them so he could slide down further into the couch. There was enough room for him to swing his legs up onto the cushion as he maneuvered himself into a lying-down position.

Micah began to move, but did not wake. Her own legs extended along his as she made herself more comfortable beside him. Her body flush against his own. He didn't care how wrong this was. It felt too right.

As he lay there with her in his arms, his mind kept drifting back to the tattoo he had briefly seen earlier. It was covered up now and there was no way he would be able to sneak a peek without waking her. It was a mystery to him. Why couldn't he figure it out?

The heart was unique. It wasn't what you would normally think of when considering a heart tattoo. It was the kind of heart you used when texting someone—a less-than sign with the number three. It formed a heart with textspeak, but why get it as a tattoo?

Then suddenly a thought came to mind. Could it be?

No. He quickly erased the thought from his mind. It was all just wishful thinking and nothing more.

Something caught his eye on the coffee table—a small stack of papers, nothing out of the ordinary. However, Drew's name stuck out at the bottom of a yellowish piece of paper, half-hidden in the pile of receipts.

Curiosity drove him to reach for it, careful not to wake Micah.

The words were hard to read in the dim evening light, but he strained to make them out. It was a love letter from Drew, and just the kick he needed in order to regain some clarity.

Micah woke some time during the night, the howling wind rousing her from a deep sleep. It took a moment for the fuzziness to fade and for her to realize just where she was sleeping, or rather, on *whom* she was sleeping.

She lifted her head from her place of comfort on Josh's chest. His breathing remained steady, a light snore escaping from his slightly opened mouth. Her legs were tangled with his as they lay entwined on the couch.

Having been best friends for so long, there had always been a level of comfort and physical affection between them, but never had she found herself in such an intimate position with him.

Her hand moved on its own accord down his chest and over his tight stomach, feeling the rippling of his hard muscles beneath the softness of his T-shirt. Her hands wanted to explore more, but her mind wouldn't let them. She couldn't accost him in his sleep. What kind of girl did something like that?

Heat warmed her cheeks, hoping he wasn't aware of her wanton behavior as he slept peacefully. Carefully, she tried to separate herself from him without waking him, moving to the chair across from the couch.

Her eyes roamed over his sleeping form. She could see the stubble on his face in the moonlight. He typically kept a shadow of a beard, tamed but not clean-shaven. It was approaching slightly scruffy and it looked good on him. Masculine. Her fingertips yearned to reach out and feel his prickly jawline.

Micah had always wondered what stubble would feel

like scraping against the softness of her own skin. Drew was so long ago, but he had always preferred a close shave. She had imagined it in her dream, but wanted to feel it for real. Just once.

His chest moved up and down in a calming rhythm as she watched, troubled by her numerous thoughts. He was such a great friend, probably even too good.

Over the years, her refusal to face her grief head-on had forced her to carry some serious baggage whether she had been aware of it or not. Her grief and pain had weighed her down like concrete set about her feet, keeping her from actually experiencing life. She had become accustomed to the weight, not fully aware of the burden it had become.

She was aware of it now. Josh had carried her the whole time, bearing the brunt of it for her. She had taken advantage of him, grown accustomed to his support. Never once had he allowed her feet to touch the ground. Never once had he insinuated that she was a burden to him. He just lovingly and willingly carried her.

Like light filling a darkened room, realization dawned on her. How could she have been so foolish? How could she have been so blind? She didn't know when it had happened, exactly, but somewhere, at some point, something had happened. It hadn't just escalated from friendship to lust. What she felt was far more intense.

Micah had fallen in love...with Josh. Once she faced the truth of it, it was all so clear. She was in love with Josh. Maybe she had always been in love with him. The knowledge both scared her and excited her. Overwhelmed her with the sudden thought of what happened next. Now that she had this new piece of information, it would change everything. She didn't want anything to change. Then again...maybe she did.

What was she thinking?

There was no way she could tell Josh about this new-found discovery. She would lose him for sure. He would never feel for her what she felt for him. This love had to stay hidden. Her relationship with Josh had always been enough before. It would still be enough.

There was no way she could go back to sleep now. Looking at the clock, she knew she had at least two more hours before daylight. She leaned back in the chair and pulled a blanket around her.

It was just too easy to keep looking at Josh as he slept. She felt like a creeper, but at the moment she didn't care. Her eyes couldn't pull away. It seemed such an intimate moment to be alone with him in the middle of the night, to see him asleep, the moonlight caressing his face.

Micah needed to find something to do if she couldn't sleep, because staring at Josh wasn't going to work. Trying to be as quiet as possible, she tiptoed to the bathroom.

She lowered the cover to the toilet seat and sat down and reached for a magazine. "How to Please Your Man" was plastered on the front cover. Thoughts filled her mind. Warmth crept up her neck and filled her cheeks. She placed a cold hand on her face to suppress the over-whelming heat taking over. She threw the magazine back down. Bad idea.

She reached for another, much tamer magazine. This was the longest night ever. The close proximity was killing her. Flipping off the light, she tiptoed back through the living room and toward the kitchen. Would she be able to make some tea without waking him?

She filled the teakettle with water and placed it on the burner. Then turned on the stove top and reached for a mug.

"Can't sleep?"

She almost dropped the mug. Spinning at the sound of his voice, she could barely see him in the darkness of the kitchen. *"You could warn a girl instead of sneaking up on her."*

"Not as much fun."

Boy, did he sound good with his early-morning sleepy voice.

Focus, Micah. Focus.

"Did I wake you?"

"Yeah, but it's no biggie." There was that voice again. Don't ask him any more questions.

"Sorry. I'm making some tea. Do you want some?"

"Sure."

Josh leaned against the kitchen wall while the water boiled. Why was it that water took so long to boil?

His hair was tousled and T-shirt rumpled. It would be so easy to take two steps and stand in front of him, rest her hands at his waist and lean into him. The way he stood practically invited her to do it. She would just have to take two steps. That's all that separated them.

She couldn't do it, though. It would ruin everything.

The hiss of the teapot caused her to jump. She turned to reach for it at the same time he did.

"Oops. Sorry."

"I can get it."

Their hands brushed up against each other, their bodies so close. She looked up at him. He looked down at her. Something in his gaze was different—fiery, full of desire.

Her eyes dropped to his lips, but the moment she realized what she had done, she knew she should turn her eyes away. Look anywhere else but at him, at his lips.

She couldn't. His tongue peeked out, quickly wetting his lips.

It happened before she even realized it was happening. She wasn't even sure if she moved first or if he did, but somehow she found her lips against his and it felt good. It was hesitant at first, slowly building. He knew what he was doing, whereas Micah...had been out of practice for a while...a long while.

Gently he backed her up until she felt the solidity of rough brick behind her. She was trapped between a wall and an immovable man. Never before had the thought of confinement been so enticing.

A heavenly rush swept through her body as his hands traveled down her sides, gripping her hips. His kiss was demanding, bruising. The rough edges of the brick wall scratched against the delicate skin of her back as his body leaned heavily against her. His fingertips dug into her flesh as he pulled her closer to him, deepening the kiss.

The intense push and pull didn't end with him. She gave back just as much. Her greedy hands slid under his shirt, fingers splayed on his strong, broad back. Desire caused her to sink her nails into his skin as she held on for dear life.

His large hands slid down her hips and gripped her thighs, lifting her up and setting her down on the kitchen counter. His hands remained on her thighs as she pulled him in closer to her. She arched her back, needing as much of her to touch as much of him as possible.

"Micah." The way he spoke her name, with such reverence, such passion, stirred her deep within.

"Say it again."

CHAPTER TWELVE

"MICAH."

She woke in a full-body sweat. Again. She pushed damp strands of hair back from her face and threw the cover off her body. Pulling herself up from the chair she had slept in, she noticed the couch across from her was vacant.

It had only been a dream.

She released the deep breath she had been holding. *Thank God.*

"Micah, you want any coffee?"

She padded to the kitchen in her slippers, the smell of coffee permeating the air. Josh looked just as he had in the dream. Her fingers tingled, itched to touch him, to run through his tousled hair, to reenact the dream still vivid in her mind.

She curled her fingers into a tight fist, bringing the errant tingling into submission. *Control yourself, woman!*

"Coffee?" Oh, his voice even sounded like she had imagined, all gravelly and rough with sleep.

"Yes, please." She sat on the barstool at the kitchen counter. He turned and set a cup of hot coffee in front of her, but avoided eye contact. That was fine with her. She couldn't have him analyzing her and finding out about her late-night musings. Her thoughts were never safe with the way he read her like a book.

"I'm gonna start clearing off my truck, then we can go pick up your car. We may have to dig it out, though."

"Okay. I'll get dressed."

Ten minutes later she found Josh outside, meticulously removing all evidence of snow from his truck. She wouldn't dare offer to help. He never let anyone touch his baby. She jumped into the cab and waited for him.

When they pulled up to the coffee-shop parking lot, her car was barely visible. It appeared to be more a giant mound of snow than a vehicle.

"This is going to be fun." Josh parked the truck and looked over at her. "You ready?"

"As ready as I will ever be."

Josh couldn't believe she didn't remember. He had walked on eggshells all morning, waiting for the awkward conversation that never came.

He looked over at her. Micah softly hummed to herself as she was hard at work on the one side of her car while he tackled the other side.

They had to shovel around the car just to get close to it. Despite the frigid temperature, Josh had worked up quite a sweat. Slowly but surely they were uncovering her little car.

He looked up at her again. She really was oblivious to what had happened last night.

Josh had woken to the sound of her walking around the apartment. It had been dark, but he'd found her in the kitchen, where she appeared to be making tea. But tea never happened.

Still in a sleepy haze, he hadn't been able to control himself and apparently neither had she. The heated make-out session had annihilated any semblance of control he thought he still possessed. Never in his wildest dreams had he expected her to be so responsive to him.

Her uninhibited passion in all of its blinding glory was far more beautiful than his finite imagination could ever have made up.

And she didn't remember a thing about it. Had she been sleepwalking? Or was it sleep kissing? Oh, God. If that was how she kissed in her sleep, he wouldn't be able to handle a kiss with her fully awake and not drunk.

Maybe this was a blessing in disguise. If she didn't remember and had truly been unaware of what transpired between them, then there was no harm done. If he could just go on as though it had never happened, she would never know.

Micah must have pushed the scraper a little too hard, because it slipped and sent snow flying into the air in his direction. He tried to duck out of its path, but failed, getting hit on the side of his face.

He couldn't pass up this opportunity. He reached down, grabbed some snow and shot back up, tossing a snowball right at her.

"Hey! We are trying to clean off the car, not put more back on it!" She countered with a snowball that just missed his shoulder.

"You started it."

Snowballs went flying through the air, rapid-fire. He threw then dodged, accidentally nailing her in the head once or twice. He felt a small pang of guilt, but got over it quickly. She would survive.

Micah hid behind the car, attempting to make as much ammunition as she could, but he was onto her. He quietly crept around the car. And as he peeked from behind the trunk, he could see her stand abruptly and fire one toward where he had been standing. She stood on her tiptoes to see if she could find him. He took the opportunity, lunged from the rear of the car and tackled her into the snow.

A spark of heat jolted him as he fell to the ground on top of her. Her body was warm beneath his, a stark contrast to the icy, wet snow that engulfed them. His face was mere inches from hers. It had started to snow again, and tiny snowflakes floated all around her.

He watched as they slowly came to rest on her hair, forming a halo about her. He was entranced by the sight of her. His mouth moved on its own accord, without permission from his mind. Lower. Lower still. Until he could taste the cotton candy lips that beckoned him.

Sweet heaven!

His entire body chose to rebel against his mind's clear commands—*hands off!* His hands didn't want to obey. They wanted to touch. His mouth wanted to consume. He wanted more. He needed more. She had turned him into a glutton—for punishment or pleasure, he wasn't sure. Maybe both.

Her lips moved in hungry response. Her fingers pushed past his hat and combed through his hair. His own hands moved to touch more, but instead of the hot flesh he was expecting, he got a handful of snow, dousing the fire immediately.

Josh jumped to his feet. "I am so sorry, Mike. I don't know what came over me."

So much for being in the clear about last night. *You weren't supposed to repeat the performance.* That ominous pit in his stomach returned with vengeance. Guilt and betrayal consumed him. When would he finally learn? The last time he'd allowed himself to get this out of control, this unguarded with Micah, horrible, unthinkable things had happened. And she had paid the price. He couldn't do it.

He could tell she was still lying in the snow, but he refused to turn. He didn't want to see the shocked expression on her face. He returned to the task at hand and cleaned off the remainder of her car as quickly as he could, fully aware of her movements as she finally stood and brushed herself off.

Josh was so disgusted with himself. He ran a rough hand over the back of his neck. He needed to get out of here. Pretend this never, ever happened.

Micah was a mess.

Her drunken kiss with Josh could be laughed off as a moment of stupidity fueled by too much tequila. Her dreams, which were so hot she feared her sheets would catch fire, could be ignored. Okay, maybe not ignored, but at least kept hidden from anyone and everyone.

But it was something else entirely when she kissed him in broad daylight in an empty parking lot without any excuse or hope of explanation. There had been no tequila to blame it on this time.

She couldn't erase from her mind the look of disgust evident on his face when he'd jumped up to get far away from her. The thought made her sick. She had made an utter fool of herself in front of the most important person in her life.

Tears pooled in her eyes before overflowing and streaming down her cheeks.

"Oh, Mikey. What's wrong?"

Micah hadn't even realized Sabina was home. She looked up at Sabina's concerned expression.

"Is it Drew?"

Why did everyone always assume it was Drew? Sure,

she still missed him. And in moments like these she missed him more than usual—not him personally, but the idea of him. It was easier to be part of a couple. You didn't have to go through as much heartbreak, like what she was experiencing now.

"You know what? There's something I need to go do."

"Okay...you want me to come with you?"

"No. I need to do this one on my own." Micah jumped up and headed to the door, grabbing her phone and purse off the counter.

"Call me if you need me."

It took a lot of courage. She had been fighting it for weeks, debating whether or not it was a good idea. But she gave in. It was something that had to be done. She had no hope of moving on until she did this.

She pulled her car slightly off the narrow drive to allow other cars to pass if they happened to come this way. She parked right in front of the sign that read Devotion and stepped out into the brisk wind.

It was a cold and dreary day. The skies were dark and gray, the clouds heavy with the possibility of rain. The weather fit the occasion.

Micah walked through the grass, up a slight hill. Her footsteps weaved a path between headstones and grave markers. The names were all familiar to her, but only because it was a path she had traveled many times.

Lowering herself to the ground, she swiped her hand across the cold, hard surface of his headstone. Her fingers gently traced each curve in his name. Stretching out, she laid her head in the grass next to the stone. It was something she had done many times before. She used to spend hours here, talking to the stone as if it could hear, as if it had a direct line to Drew's ear. She had always been so desperate for a connection. Something. Anything.

Micah had something to say to him now, and this had been the only place she could think of to do it. It seemed appropriate for a final goodbye. The last few months had been rough. She had gone from one extreme to the other, trying to find a middle ground with her emotions.

It was time—time to let it all go.

She inhaled deeply, breathing in the cool air, allowing it to calm her tumultuous heart. The ground below her was cold and hard, but she remained there, wanting to be close to him one last time.

"Drew..." She spoke out loud to nothing but marble. "I've decided that it's time I let you go. I don't want to be in denial any longer or remain captive to memories of you. I don't want to feel this anger and bitterness or this pain and loss anymore. Instead, I choose to accept the fact that you are gone. That that chapter of my life is long over and it's time to look forward. I want to remember the good. You were a good man and you were good to me. I want to think back on you as a fond memory. I've loved you for most of my life and I know a part of me always will. But it's time. I need to move on and make some new memories of my own."

She stayed there for a moment longer, letting it all sink in. She sat up, ran her hand across his name one more time. "Goodbye, Drew."

Rain began to fall, soft at first. It splashed on her cheek and mingled with her tears. She felt it glide down her face and drop to her chest. It was silly, but she had always considered rain to be a sign from the heavens. It was as if Drew was responding, letting her go, finally.

She stood there in a place of previous devotion and let the rain envelop her. Turning her face up to the sky, she allowed the drops to cleanse her of the wreckage and the grief that had consumed her.

Peace. She felt peace.

Feeling lighter than she had in years, Micah headed home. Of course, she hadn't solved all her problems, but at least she was free of the burden that had weighed her down for so long.

As she walked in the door, Sabina must have noticed the bounce in her step, too. "Well, whatever errand you just ran must have helped."

"Yes. It did."

"Good."

Micah's phone chirped. Incoming text message.

Can we pretend this morning never happened?

It was from Josh. That was easy for him to say. Her phone chirped again.

I don't know what happened. I'm the worst friend ever. Forgive me?

Should she just go with it, pretend she hadn't gotten a small taste of heaven this morning? If she did it might rescue their quickly sinking friendship. If she didn't, would she be saying goodbye to him, too?

"Hey, Jamie will be here in, like, an hour. Wants to do coffee if you want to come." Sabina interrupted her thoughts.

"Um, yeah. Sure."

She looked back down at Josh's text, torn.

One goodbye was enough for today.

All's forgiven and forgotten. Don't even know what you
are talking about.

Her phone signaled another message.

You're the best <3

An hour later she sat at a table surrounded by her
friends in their favorite little coffee shop.

"Did Josh have to work?" Hanna asked as she blew
on her steaming cup of coffee.

"Yeah. He got called in at the last minute." Leave it
to Micah to be the only one who knew Josh's comings
and goings. Did anyone see the oddity in that? She was
mortified if so. No one needed to know the feelings she
now possessed. They were to remain under lock and key.

"What a shame. I haven't seen him since the party."

"Well, with your schedule it's no wonder you get to
see anyone."

"You're right. But I can't slow down now. I am finally
getting somewhere with my career. I can slow down when
I'm dead."

Micah took a tentative sip of her coffee.

"Hey, what did you guys think of Josh's new girlfriend?"

Micah almost choked. Leave it to Sabina to go there.

"Her name is Taylor." Jamie, leaning back against the
window, spoke casually, as if the one statement were
self-explanatory.

"So?" The three girls all looked at one another in puz-
zlement.

"So...if they get married she would be Taylor Taylor."

They all broke out in laughter, Micah forcing a laugh

so as not to stand out. It was a little funny to think about, if she ignored the part about him getting married.

"I don't think anyone has to worry about that." Hanna waved a hand dismissively. "He goes through women just as often as Sabina goes through men."

"Hey, that hurts." Sabina swatted at her.

Jamie ignored them. "Are you sure? She's different. She seems more like the type he could settle down with. She seemed really sweet, unlike most of the women he dates."

Micah sat quietly as her friends, unaware of her rising panic, talked around her. Was Josh really serious about this girl? It was one thing to say she would be okay with a lifetime of friendship. She didn't want to sit on the sidelines secretly in love with her best friend while watching him fall for someone else. It would be torture to watch him marry and build a life with another woman.

Her friends continued to talk about the girls in Josh's past, starting with the ones they'd disliked the most. There was the model, the doctor, the cheerleader, the makeup artist…oh, and they didn't forget the pageant queen!

As if she needed to be reminded again of just how little chance she had of being the object of his desire.

Micah slammed her cup down on the table, effectively ending the conversation. Three sets of eyes snapped to attention.

"Hanna, what was that guy's name? The one you introduced me to at the party?" Micah needed to move on from Josh, too. She couldn't take a giant step forward in one area of her life only to remain where she felt most comfortable in another area. She had wasted enough of her life stuck in the past. It was time to live.

"Heck, yeah! Mr. Tall Drink of Water!" Sabina bounced in her chair.

"Cameron?" Hanna looked puzzled by the quick change in conversation.

"Yes. Him. You still have his number?"

"Sure."

"He's still single, right?"

"You met him a week ago. He was single then. I'm almost positive he'll still be single this week."

"Good."

She had shocked all of them. They knew she was trying to move on, but they hadn't expected this any more than she had.

CHAPTER THIRTEEN

"When does Cameron get here?"

Sabina leaned against the bathroom door as Micah put on the finishing touches to her makeup. Micah could see it in her eyes, she was evaluating her outfit and judging whether it was dateworthy enough. Well, Micah liked the way she looked and that was all that mattered.

"He should be here any minute now."

"Where is he taking you?"

"We are going out to dinner. I'm not sure where." She opened her eyes wide to apply the last coat of mascara, her mouth opening as well. She found it humorous that her mouth always opened when she applied eye makeup. It made no sense whatsoever.

"Here, wear these."

Sabina held out a pair of giant turquoise earrings. They were beautiful, but they weren't her. No use putting up a false front with this guy. She wasn't Sabina and never would be. From here on out, she would wear what she wanted and do what she wanted and no longer allow people to make decisions for her, regardless of how much she loved them.

"No. I think I prefer these."

"Suit yourself."

Yes. It did suit her. Micah. The one and only.

It felt good to be herself, to actually know who she was for the first time in, like...well, ever.

Micah glanced at her phone for the zillionth time that day. No new messages. Each time she looked, her heart broke a little more. It shouldn't. She should be past this by now. She had come to accept his friendship and nothing more. But part of her had hoped he would call, hoped he would hear about her date and rush in to stop her. Apparently, she had watched one too many chick flicks.

She gave herself a final look in her full-length mirror. She had bought a new dress just for tonight. When she saw it in the store, she had to have it. She had seen something like it in a magazine; a celebrity had worn it to an event and had everyone talking. It was a new look they called color blocking—the dress itself was black, but curved white inserts in the center front and center back gave the illusion of a smaller and much curvier shape. The moment she tried it on, she had felt sexier than ever before. It was unbelievable just how one dress could transform how she viewed herself.

She had painstakingly flat-ironed her hair, a rare occurrence for her riotous curls. This date was special, the first date in ten years that she was actually going to give a chance. She felt it was deserving of the added effort.

There was a knock at the door. Her stomach churned with nervous first-date jitters. This had to be a severe case. Sabina answered and let him in. "Micah, Cameron's here."

As if she couldn't hear him from her room five feet away from the front door. *Silly girl.* He was wearing a sharp gray suit. Not the typical business suit, though, it was more tailored, as though he had just stepped from the pages of an Express catalog or something. He looked good in it, too. His dark hair was styled nicely with pomade.

"You look nice." His face broke out into a big grin when she walked in.

"Thank you." It had been too long since a guy had smiled like that because of her. And it was even better with Sabina standing next to her.

She really needed to get over her insecurity of being near Sabina. They were both different and unique and beautiful in their own ways. And Micah had a lot to offer! It was about time she figured that out.

"Ready?"

Oh, jeez. This was nerve-racking. Could she survive this night? The last minute second-guessing commenced. Should she even go? She gazed up at his smiling, kind and well-groomed face. *Heck, yeah!* "Yes."

"Have fun, kids." Sabina waved like a fool as they walked into the hallway. How embarrassing. Micah rolled her eyes, but couldn't help but laugh. Sabina would get it later.

He opened the door to his silver BMW. *Chivalrous.* She took note of that. All her life she had surrounded herself with guys who knew how to treat a lady. She wouldn't settle for less. *Calm down there, Micah. No one is asking you to settle down just yet.*

He took her to a beautiful restaurant in downtown Boston, one she would never be able to afford. She had always looked at it with wonder, hoping to sample the fine dining it had to offer one day.

Now that she actually walked through the front doors and was given a seat at a highly sought-after table, she felt out of place. It was too nice for her. She wasn't sure how to act, but Cameron put her at ease. He wasn't up-pity or snobby, just normal and easygoing, easy to talk to. Conversation flowed naturally between the two of them.

They talked about his work, in the same offices where

Hanna worked. He asked about the job she was about to start and seemed interested in it. She found out he came from a large family in Missouri, of all places. She had been wondering about his strange accent, but didn't want to say anything because he would only tease her about hers. The Boston accent was difficult to cover up.

Everything was going so well. She felt happy. She felt confident. She no longer thought about her insecurities or where she fell short.

She felt like the old Micah, or better yet, a new Micah. A brand-new, never-before-seen version of herself. And it felt great. She smiled as she thought about how far she had come in such a short time.

"What? Did I say something?" Cameron's question broke through her musings. She had forgotten about him for a moment.

Oops.

"Oh, sorry. No. Nothing you said. Just a silly thought. Nothing, really. My apologies. What were you saying?"

"I was just talking about Boston sports."

"Ooh, love 'em."

"I was saying how I didn't get into them."

"Are you serious?"

He laughed. "Yes."

"How can this be? How can you live in Boston and not enjoy all the sports we have to offer? We have the best of everything all rolled into one fine city."

"It's easy. I just don't."

"I'm floored. There's not a single sport you get into? We've got it all."

He shook his head, laughing at her reaction.

"Well, what kind of sports do you play in Missouri?"

"I don't know. I never got into sports there, either."

"You, sir, are quite the enigma. I just never knew it was possible."

"Since you obviously feel differently than I do, what sports do you watch?"

"I watch them all. My friends try to all get together to have game days or game nights, whatever the sport. We're watching football right now, obviously."

"You get together for every game?"

"Yeah, we try to at least. It happens most of the time. It's easy for some of us, but poor Jamie lives outside the city, so he has quite a drive every week. But he's faithful."

"You guys sound like an episode of *Friends*."

"Ha, you're right! We do! Although none of us has slept together...that I know of, anyway."

They both laughed for a moment as the waiter came to serve their food and refill their wine.

As he walked her to her door later that night, her mind was racing. Her heartbeat quickened when he bent. Thankfully, his lips landed on her cheek and not her lips.

As she closed the door, she couldn't help but wonder why she hadn't wanted him to kiss her. They'd had fun. They had enjoyed their time together. He was great-looking, unbelievably kind and intelligent. What more could she want?

She wanted butterflies. Not just predate jitters. Was that crazy? Was she being stupid? Too picky?

"Hey. How did it go?" Sabina was waiting for her on the couch. It was actually quite cute since it was such a role reversal—Sabina was typically out every night, so staying in to wait to hear how her friend's date went was something new for her. "Come sit down. Tell me everything. I want to know all the juicy details."

"It went well." Micah put down her purse, took off her jacket and sat down on the couch.

"Do you think he'll ask you out on a second date?"

"Maybe."

"And would you say yes to a second date?"

"I don't know. Maybe."

"That didn't sound very convincing. What was wrong? He was cute. He seemed really nice. I know for a fact he has a great job. Does he have some kind of weird fetish or does he eat with his mouth open?"

"What? No. Neither of those things."

"Then what is it?"

"I don't know. I can't put my finger on it. Just something wasn't right."

"I'm proud of you."

"For what?"

"For going out and taking this giant step, this leap into a world you've let pass you by for far too long. You'll find someone eventually. I know you will. You have too much to offer someone."

Why were her friends always so hard to find when she really needed them? She needed someone to talk to, and she would prefer Sabina. Where was she, anyway?

Micah paced the living room. She was in desperate need of advice, and no one was around to give it to her. Hanna was too caught up in her blissfully happy wedding plans. Jamie was busy. And Josh...well, Josh was the one she needed advice about. She couldn't very well ask him about him.

She had been foolish to believe one date with someone else could cure her of the feelings that had slowly been developing over the course of a decade. She just needed to talk to someone about it. Keeping it hidden from everyone was only making it worse. If she didn't vent about it soon, she'd explode.

She pulled out her phone and sent Sabina a quick text.

Where are you?

Sabina texted back right away.

I'm at the movies with Jordan.

It would be at least two hours before she came home. Micah didn't know if she could wait that long. She could just text Sabina about her problem. That would work.

No. Bad idea.

She put her phone down on the table and walked away. Maybe a shower would help put things in perspective. It was quite possible she might be able to solve her own predicament.

One long, hot shower later and she was still nowhere closer to an answer to her problem. She pulled her robe tight around her as she picked up her phone, once again debating whether to go ahead and text Sabina or not. The familiar ping sounded, signifying a new message. Josh.

Guess who's playing at House of Blues this weekend.

For days she had longed for some form of communication from this man and *now* was the time he chose?

Ah! She needed Sabina's advice and she couldn't wait any longer. She couldn't keep ignoring the Josh situation. So she grabbed a hold of her phone and started typing.

Bina, I don't know what to do. I need to talk to you and I don't think I can wait until you get home. Ah! I think I have feelings for Josh. Like falling-in-love feelings. Like more-than-friends feelings. What should I do?

She hit the send button, the zip sound echoing in the quiet apartment. It was the first time she had "voiced" the words. It made her nervous to admit it to anyone other than herself. It made it real. Her eyes scanned the text again.

No! No! No!

There, at the top of the text message where Sabina's name should be prominently displayed was another name entirely. The one and only name she had been purposely avoiding. She had accidentally sent the message to Josh! There was no way she could talk herself out of this one. No way to retrieve it now, either.

Making sure she was actually texting Sabina this time, she typed out the words Emergency! Get home now! Pushing the phone away, she sat at a distance, staring at it. Had he read it yet?

It rang, her heart stopped, her breathing coming in short frantic breaths. She inched toward the phone, the happy jingle sounding shrill to her ears.

Sabina. Thank God. She hit the accept button.

"Micah, are you okay? What's wrong? Do you need to call 911?" Sabina's words came out in a panicked rush.

"It's not a 911 emergency. It's a friend emergency. It's awful! I don't know what to do! I think I just ruined everything! Actually, I know I just ruined everything!"

"Okay. Slow down. What are you talking about?"

"I needed advice so I was going to text you and ask you what I should do."

"Then ask me."

"Well, see, it's more than that…. See, I think I'm falling in love with Josh."

"Oh…my…gosh…"

"It gets worse. I accidentally texted him instead of you."

"What did the text say?"

"It said just that—that I was falling in love with him. What am I going to do? I am so embarrassed! I don't think I can recover from this. You may need to start looking for a new roommate, because I'm gonna have to move out of state."

"Okay. I'm heading home now, but he'll probably call you or text you before I get there."

"I can't talk to him right now! I was texting you to find out how to handle this." The emotion was overwhelming; she couldn't control the tears as they fell down her cheeks. "I'm not ready to talk to him yet. I don't think I'll ever be ready for this conversation."

"Just ignore him until I get home. That way I'll be there to hold your hand when you do take his call."

"What have I done?"

"Stop getting yourself so worked up. Make yourself some tea and just sit tight until I get there."

Micah hung up the phone and went about making some chamomile tea as Sabina had suggested.

Josh still hadn't responded. Either he hadn't received it or he was in shock and didn't know how to respond. She had really messed this one up badly. Stupid. Stupid. Stupid.

The tea did nothing to calm her. She kept putting her phone down, just to pick it up again. No new messages. The stress of it all was going to be the death of her.

Knock. Knock.

CHAPTER FOURTEEN

MICAH'S BODY WENT RIGID. Sabina had a key. It was her apartment. She wouldn't knock. Micah knew who it was and the thought of answering the door made her start to sweat. She could ignore it.

"Micah?" He yelled through the door, confirming her suspicion. She remained frozen, hoping he would go away.

"Micah, I know you're in there. I saw your light on."

She could have left her light on. It didn't mean she was here.

"We need to talk. Please, just let me in."

Go away!

"I can just talk through the door if you prefer. Not sure if your neighbors will be too happy about that, though."

Her neighbors would hate it. Besides, it was none of their business.

"Micah, please. I need to talk to you. I need to see your face."

She couldn't help herself, peeking through the door's peephole. He looked the way she felt. He ran his hand through his hair, which looked as though it had seen better days. She rested her forehead on the cold door, letting out a deep breath she hadn't been aware she was holding. She couldn't face him. She just couldn't do it.

"I can hear you breathing and can see the shadow of your feet. Please. Just open the door."

Her hand rested on the cool metal of the doorknob. She couldn't face him, but couldn't help responding to him, either. "You weren't supposed to get that."

"I gathered that much."

"I'm so sorry, Josh."

"Open the door, Micah. Sorry for what?"

"For ruining everything. I've messed it all up." She turned the knob and slowly opened the door, standing back to let him in.

"Micah." His eyes brimmed with pain and indecision. She knew whatever words came out of his mouth would hurt her. They would cut like a knife. Even her name on his lips sliced through her.

"Don't. Don't say it." She couldn't bear to look into his eyes anymore. The words came out on a whisper, too difficult to say. "I don't think I can handle it."

"It's just that… Micah, I still see you as Drew's. I think I'll always see you that way…off-limits. He was one of my best friends. I have to honor his memory in this."

She spun at his words, a spark igniting within her. How dare he? She spoke through clenched teeth. "He's gone, Josh. His claim on me died with him."

"But still—"

She cut him off. He'd hear her out even if it was the last she ever said to him. "As my friend, do you really think that's fair to me? To condemn me to a life of lone-liness because *once* I belonged to someone who is now dead? Is that what you hope for me? Is that all you see happening in my future? Because I'm considered un-touchable to you?"

Micah walked to the window, her eyes unable to take anything in but the snowy-white abyss that lay beyond.

Her tone softened after she took a deep, calming breath, her back to him. "Drew *was* my first love. That place in my heart will always belong to him. But what we had, although real, was nothing more than teenage love. Even if that accident hadn't happened, I honestly don't think we would have lasted much longer. No matter how much I have imagined it."

She pulled the edges of her robe tighter, needing its comfort and warmth. "For the last ten years, I've desperately held on to a memory, an idea. I fooled myself into believing that my life was pointless without him, that any hope of a happy future had died with him. But it was all lies that I told myself to put off the grieving process. I had become comfortable in my denial. It felt safer than the alternative, which was to put myself back out there, susceptible to heartbreak again. Sure, I went through the motions. I appeared to be normal, happy and healthy to the naked eye. But deep inside of me, hidden from sight, lay this ticking time bomb that just waited for the perfect moment to explode. That semblance of *normal* life blown to smithereens, leaving me wounded and gaping and empty."

Micah paused; silence echoed throughout the room. Josh hadn't said a word, nor had he made a move. But she could feel his presence. Slowly she turned, looking him straight in the eye. "I've put him to rest. I've faced my inner demons head-on. I have fought my way through denial, depression, anger and bitterness. I have battled it out with the memories and ghosts that haunted me. And after I won, I locked the past away once and for all. I've finally found acceptance and peace and *freedom*. So don't you dare tell me that I am still bound by a man long since dead! He's controlled my life from the grave for far too long. But not anymore."

She took another deep breath. Her knees felt weak, but she ignored them, gathered her nerve and stood up straighter. He would not see an ounce of weakness in her. Not if she could do anything about it.

"I survived Drew. I can survive you, too. I deserve more. I deserve a life full of love and happiness. I've missed out on that and I won't let myself continue down that road. I want to stop thinking about what I've missed out on and start thinking about what lies ahead. So I guess the real question is—will you be a part of my future, Josh, or just a part of my past?"

He stood there. Just stood there! Immovable. And every second that passed felt like an eternity. Each moment caused another crack to form in the fragile armor she held up around her heart, threatening to shatter it into tiny irretrievable pieces.

His words were barely audible, but her heart knew before her ears were able to translate to her brain. "I… can't…"

Her vision glazed over as she stood frozen in her heartbreak, not even aware of his quiet exit out of her apartment, and out of her life.

She was experiencing a new grief, a different kind of grief. This was altogether suffocating and confining. She felt it close in on her like a heavy weight.

No!

She wouldn't allow this to happen again.

Micah straightened her shoulders and dragged a hand across her face, wiping the tears from her eyes.

She would allow herself a good cry, and maybe a pint or two of Ben & Jerry's, but enough was enough. If he chose to walk away, then it was his loss. She would not be held under the law of his gravity. She had tasted freedom and the possibility of a new life. Nothing would get in her way. She was stronger than this.

Sabina arrived and after a sob-filled account of the last ten minutes they shared the ice cream while Micah continued to cry. Sabina talked her into a movie completely free of any romance.

But five minutes in a phone rang. Micah lunged for it, hoping it was Josh. Disappointed to find it wasn't even her phone ringing.

Sabina answered and mouthed Hanna's name. Her brows began to knit together in a frown. It was the only time Micah had seen Sabina's face look slightly unpretty—far from being ugly, just a little *not* pretty. The thought brought a smile to her tear-streaked face before she realized that Sabina was frowning, which was a cause for concern. Afraid it might cause wrinkles, she didn't frown very often.

"What's wrong?"

Sabina held up a finger, signaling her to wait a moment. Which she did, even if it was done rather impatiently.

"Hanna just caught Nathan in bed with another woman. Come on. Let's go."

"What?" She hurried to find her boots and coat as she made sense of it. "She has to be devastated. We'll need to pick up a lot more Ben & Jerry's."

"And maybe some wine."

"Or something harder."

"You're right."

They drove quickly to Hanna's house. As they entered, they noticed a couple of broken vases, or possibly plates, littering the floor, evidence of Hanna's well-known temper.

"Hanna, what happened?" She looked awful, mascara streaks marring her face.

"He's been cheating on me! All this time I thought he was working late like I was, but no. He's been hooking up with an associate!"

"Did he tell you how long it's been going on?" Micah was afraid to speak, did not want to further upset Hanna, but maybe talking about it would get her to calm down a little. She wrapped her arm around Hanna's back and began to rub up and down in an effort to calm her.

"Yeah. I forced it out of him. He says he has been with her for a while. Apparently it started not long after we first got together. Can you believe that? How stupid am I? How could I not see this? I fell for all his crap, bought a house with him and was planning to marry him. I even bought a dress last week!"

"You did?" Sabina asked and Micah sent her a look that said *not now.* The fact that she'd gone wedding-dress shopping without them was irrelevant now—hurtful, but irrelevant.

"I'm so sorry, Han. I never did think he was deserving of you. I know you probably do not want to hear it right now, but it really is a good thing that you didn't marry him. You got to see him for who he really is before saying *I do.*" Micah tried to reassure her.

"And the better news is we brought ice cream and Bailey's," Sabina piped in, holding up the bottle and carton for Hanna to see. "It may not solve your problems, but it will make you happier for tonight, at least."

"Aw, thanks, guys. I'm so glad you came to my rescue." The tears flowed again as Hanna wrapped her arms around each of them. "I don't know what I would do without you."

"You will never have to find out."

"We will take good care of you. Now let the man-hating party begin!" Sabina said as she made her way to the kitchen. They would need spoons. These girls had no need for bowls or glasses during a man-hating party. They drank straight from the bottle and ate straight from the carton during times like this. Helping Hanna through her pain had a way of helping Micah forget her own. It had been a full half hour since the last time she had thought about Josh. They would each get through this and be stronger because of it.

When Josh had closed Micah's door behind him, he knew it would be the moment he would look back on with regret for the rest of his life. Two words would haunt him for the rest of his days.

I. Can't.

He had wanted to rush back in there, tell her what a coward and liar he was, but there was still a part of him that hadn't let him. Something that drove his feet to move, step by step, farther and farther away from her door.

The real truth, the gut-wrenching reality, had been right there in the middle of her heartfelt speech.

She deserved more.

Micah would never know the reasons why he had to walk away. If she ever did find out, she would never forgive him, making a relationship impossible. It was for the best. He just had to keep telling himself that.

CHAPTER FIFTEEN

THE DAYS THAT followed were lonely and quiet without Josh. She hated it. Even though they did not see each other on a daily basis, he used to call or text her every day. But she hadn't heard from him. Not since that night.

It was for the best. She needed to learn to get on without him. She needed to learn how to do this on her own, to be independent and gain confidence outside of a man's attention and affection.

She had learned so much about herself recently. Her eyes had been opened for the first time in years. She had spent all of that time dependent on Drew and Josh.

His rejection was a good thing. It did not feel that way at first, but she was seeing it now. She did not recognize the girl she used to be anymore. She would always be grateful for all that Josh had done to help her get past that.

It was sad losing that relationship, but she was excited to see what the future held. Her options for a happy future were limitless. She now had the confidence and independence to make it happen.

"He still hasn't called?" Sabina's question knocked her from her thoughts. Micah had not realized she was staring at her phone without seeing.

"No, but it's all right. I think it is for the best."

"How so?"

"I need to learn to survive without a man."

"Do you, now?" Sabina arched her eyebrow and pursed her lips in the infamous duck face. "Who are you and what have you done with my bestie?"

"What are you talking about? I am here. I have always been here."

"Well, physically you have been, but I feel like you have been gone from me for a while. I have seen glimpses of the Micah I love, but it has been a long, long time."

"Yeah. I know."

"You have had a difficult year."

"It really has been a rough year. I don't know why it became more difficult for me, but I know it was for a reason. It all came to a peak, and I was forced to face reality. I needed that. I needed to deal with the past and finally put it all behind me."

"Good. It is so nice to hear you talk like that." Sabina stood and smoothed out her pant legs. "You ready for this?"

"As ready as I will ever be." Micah had been dreading this for a few days now. They were all meeting at Hanna's to help her move.

The girls would arrive first so they could help pack the boxes. Then the guys would show up later with the truck and load it up. That helped a little. She wouldn't know how to act if Josh arrived there first and she showed up later. It would put pressure on her to say something, do something. If she was there first, then she could be busy doing things by the time he arrived. Seemed like a good enough plan.

She grabbed her coat and followed Sabina out the door. *Here goes nothing.*

Micah was in the bedroom packing up all of Hanna's personal items when she heard the guys arrive. Her heart began to pound. Her hands began to shake. She kept folding and packing, doing her best to concentrate on the clothing and not on what was happening downstairs.

It didn't work. She could hear his voice as he laughed. He sounded good. Did he miss her? Did her absence affect him in any way? Or had he just gone on the way he always did when women came in and out of his life? She had always thought she was different. Was she now just another one of them?

Furniture banged against something. "Hey, watch the furniture! You are going to pay for anything you damage, boys!"

Micah laughed as she imagined the scene. Two guys with their muscles, sweating, lifting heavy objects...

Whoa!

Her mind was going places it should not. Hanna was probably standing on the staircase watching their every move, directing them and being her overcautious self, making sure her furniture was moved unscathed.

Footsteps sounded on the stairs, then down the hallway. She knew whom they belonged to without even seeing him. He turned the corner into the room.

A simple gray T-shirt had never looked so good. Long, muscular legs encased in old, worn-out jeans. His hair messed up just so. *Gawd,* he looked good.

She felt her heart breaking all over again. They were supposed to do this run-in with others around. It would have been easier that way. Why couldn't it have worked out that way?

"Hi."

All he had to do was say one word and it was her undoing. She had no idea how she did not collapse into a mess of tears, but she was able to manage a smile. She could do this. She knew she could.

"Hanna wanted me to start grabbing some boxes to shove up on top in the moving truck. Do you have any that are ready?"

"Those are." Two words. Good enough. She pointed to the boxes near the door, but he just continued to look at her. She could see his heart in his eyes and it looked just as broken as hers. *Please leave so I can cry in peace.*

She really should have come up with an excuse for not being able to help today. She hadn't told Hanna about her recent developments because she had her own problems to work through. She didn't need Micah's drama, too. Hanna needed her help. She could get past her own issues in order to help her friend. She could and she would.

He finally made his way to the boxes, stacking one on top of the other and lifting them both at the same time. It would make this go a lot faster if he could manage carrying multiples. He quickly glanced back one more time before disappearing through the doorway.

Micah hurried to finish her duties. Just get the boxes packed and she could get out of there, away from the reminders of all she had lost and all she would never have. With her back to the door, she worked hard and kept the tears at bay. She didn't want to see Josh each time he retrieved more boxes. Thankfully, that was only two more times. Both times she made herself busy.

She could sense him standing there, watching her. Slowly, she turned. He stood in the doorway with his hands in his pockets.

"I'm sorry, Mike."

"Don't."

"I never meant—"

"Please stop." She took a deep breath and stared at the shirt she had been in the process of folding. "I didn't think… I mean, I never thought this would happen. I never expected it to. I always assumed you would be there. I took you for granted, took our friendship for granted. I'm sorry."

"You didn't—"

"No. Stop. I know we can never go back to how it used to be, but I'm hoping we can at least be somewhat normal around one another. Do you think that's possible?"

He stared down at his feet, avoiding eye contact. Silence stretched between them before he finally spoke. "Yeah. We can do that."

His shoulders dropped slightly as he turned to leave. Micah stared at the empty doorway, unable to fathom how this relationship had crumbled so quickly. It hadn't been as indestructible as they'd assumed it was.

"How's it going up here?"

Micah turned to see Hanna enter. Her eyes must have given her away, because Hanna's filled with concern as she came closer. Hanna rested her hand on Micah's, hindering her progress. "What's going on, Micah? Is something wrong?"

"No. I'm fine. I'm almost finished."

"Forget the stuff, Micah. Stop. Sit down. Tell me. What's the matter? And don't bother denying it. I can read you like a book."

"It's not..." Hanna's eyebrow lifted up, halting her ensuing denial. "Fine. I did something stupid and now things are really messed up with Josh, and I just want to go home."

"What did you do? Oh, please tell me one of you finally confessed your true feelings!"

"What?"

"I have been waiting for years for one of you to come to your senses."

"Why haven't you said anything?"

"Neither of you was ready to hear it. But stop avoiding the question. What did you do?"

"I realized…"

"Yes?"

"…that…I've fallen in love with Josh."

"It's about time."

"I don't know what you are talking about."

"So what did you do?"

"I accidentally told him."

"What do you mean, *accidentally?*"

"Well, I meant to text Sabina about it, but I had an oops moment and sent it to Josh instead."

"Classic."

"How can you be so casual about this?"

"Because you guys are meant to be together. Everyone knows that."

"No. No one knows that."

"So, what happened?" Hanna was relentless.

"He doesn't feel the same."

"That's what he said?"

"His exact words were *I can't.*"

"Aw, Micah. I'm sorry it went down like that. Give it time. I know you two are meant to be together, and it will all work out eventually."

Micah stood, dragged her hands across her face and wiped the leftover tears on her jeans. She looked down at the things that still needed to be packed. "Let's stop worrying about me and keep working on getting you out of here."

"You're right. I need to end this chapter of my life as soon as possible. Get back to work."

Josh reclined on his couch. His once comfortable apartment now seemed barren and lonely. Everywhere he looked he was reminded of her. She had been woven into every area of his life. He just didn't function without her.

It had been so painful to see her today and know that he was the one responsible for the hurt in her eyes. He wanted to hold her, to make it all better, but he couldn't.

The pit in his stomach made itself known. He could remember that night so vividly, the paralyzing guilt from the part he played still fresh. The night he'd vowed to protect Micah. The night she'd permanently become off-limits.

Josh had just pulled into his driveway when his phone rang. It was Drew and he knew exactly what the impending conversation was going to be about. They had spent the evening celebrating Drew's birthday before the rain had scattered them and forced them all to go home. By this point, Drew must have just dropped off Micah, finally freeing him up to call and let Josh have it.

He was tempted to not answer, but curiosity won.

"Hello?"

"Dude, what's your problem?" Yup. He was mad.

"What are you talking about?"

"Don't pull that with me, Josh. You know exactly what I'm talking about. What the hell?"

This was a conversation they revisited every couple of months. Josh would forget himself and Drew would catch him staring at Micah. He couldn't help it. She was a beautiful girl.

"I don't see what the big deal is. I was only looking. It's not like I've ever touched her."

"And you never will. Get that through your thick skull. She's mine! And she'll always be mine!"

"I know. I know."

"Oh, damn! No! No!"

Josh held the phone close to his ear, straining to hear

what was happening, but the rain pounding on his wind-shield made it difficult. "Drew?"

Everything was muffled, but the sound of screeching tires was unmistakable. It all happened so quickly that Josh couldn't distinguish one thing from another. The horrifying sounds of twisting metal and shattering glass pierced through the phone, like nothing he had ever heard before. His breathing halted, his heart rate plummeted. It was as if everything ceased to function in that moment. Then, just as suddenly as it had happened, an eerie silence filled the air.

Panic consumed him. "Drew! Talk to me, man!"

It was faint but he could hear a moan, a painful cry, something.

"Drew, where are you? What happened? Drew, talk to me!"

"Josh." It was barely audible, but it was something.

"I'm coming, man. Where are you?"

"No." The word sounded weak, a gasping sound rather than a command. "Promise..."

"Drew—"

Josh strained to hear around the pounding of his own heartbeat.

"Micah..."

"Anything. I'll do anything, Drew. I'll protect her, even from me."

It was alarmingly quiet, except for a muffled gurgling sound and erratic heaving breaths. He didn't know what to do. Drew was in distress and he had no idea where he was or what had happened. He would have told Drew anything at that moment just to keep him calm.

"I promise, Drew. She'll always be yours."

The silence that followed was deafening.

No!

The magnitude of what had just happened hit Josh with a leveling force. His head fell forward onto the steering wheel, a gut-wrenching cry of pain escaping from deep within.

CHAPTER SIXTEEN

IT WAS THE start of a new day, a new chapter in her life. It had been far too long since she had put her knowledge to work, but now it was time. After being a nanny for the last several years, she worried if she still had what it took.

After the girls helped her shop for some new clothes, she felt superconfident. She definitely would not be taken seriously if she showed up in the same clothes she had worn as a nanny—her nanny family had not even taken her seriously when she showed up in those clothes.

She had selected a basic black pencil skirt, but her newfound curves were amplified in this baby. Even though she had put on a little weight, she actually liked the result and could not remember the last time she had felt this confident.

She grabbed her stylish new satchel purse and headed out the door, her new confidence marking her stride. *Watch out, business world. I'm about to take over.*

It felt good to be taken seriously again. Felt good to have something to contribute. And basically…she felt good.

When Micah entered her new work environment, her soon-to-be coworkers sized her up and tossed her looks of competition. *Bring it on! Bring it on!* Okay, so maybe she was getting a little out of control, her head growing with each step she took.

There was a tiny voice in her head that caused her to second-guess herself momentarily. Old habits had a tendency of dying hard, but she quickly stomped the negative thoughts from her mind. She would remain positive from here on out. She would not allow negativity to hold her back any longer. She was a changed woman, and she was bound to make that a permanent change.

After a few hours of initial training, she was given a break. In desperate need of a coffee, she grabbed her purse and headed out the door. Decisions, decisions. To the left, past the firehouse where Josh worked, was a coffee shop. Or she could go to the right and across the street.

Her positive, confident outlook pushed her to the left. The trucks were parked out front; several firemen cluttered the area. Josh had to be there. Somewhere. *You look good in that skirt. Strut past that firehouse and show him what he's missing.*

Yup, no. She wasn't *that* confident. She turned sharply to the right and made a beeline across the street.

"Where is everyone?" Jamie walked into Josh's apartment expecting the regular people in attendance but instead was faced with an empty room.

"Oh, uh…Hanna's working."

"On Sundays now?"

"Guess so."

"And the others?"

"Sabina is mad at me…"

"And Micah?"

Josh didn't say anything. The silence was answer enough.

"What happened?" Jamie asked as he settled into his favorite spot on Josh's couch and propped his feet up on the coffee table.

"You want me to grab you a beer before I get into it?"

"Yeah."

Josh went into the kitchen, opened the refrigerator and pulled out two. He popped the tops off and handed one to Jamie when he returned to the living room, and settled down into his own seat after.

"Okay, spill. What happened?"

"So much…"

"Start from the beginning."

"Nah, man. I don't want to revisit all that."

"Give me the bullet-points version, then."

"Well…I was a fool. I took advantage of her when she was drunk. I lost all sense of self-control, cared more about my own lust… I treated her like just another girl I'd pick up in a bar."

Jamie leaned back in his seat and propped his ankle on the opposite knee. "Continue."

"Then I get this text the other day…"

"Yeah?"

"Mind you, this is after I lost all control." Josh took another swig of his beer. "But this text…I guess she meant to send it someone else. It was obvious it was never meant for me to see."

"Oh, really? That's happened to me before. What did it say?"

"Basically it just said she had feelings for me."

"What? That's awesome. That makes it so much easier for you now." Jamie took a sip of his beer. Then, as if he had thought about it a moment, he sat up straighter. "Wait. Now I am confused. Why isn't she here then? I thought you were in love with her. Shouldn't she be here playing kissy face with you now that the secret is out?"

"It's complicated."

"Well, uncomplicate it for me."

"I *am* in love with her. That's a given. But I can't be with her."

"That doesn't make any sense. Why not?"

"I thought we talked about this."

"We did, but I'm still not seeing it."

"She belongs to Drew. She always will be hands off to me. Our friendship means too much to me to muck it up."

"So what has happened now hasn't already mucked it up? I mean, look around. You still lost her."

"I guess no matter what I do, I lose. At least this way I have the hope that she will find someone better than me and will eventually forgive me."

"Are you kidding me? Who could possibly be a better match for her than you?"

"Tons of guys."

"You're full of it!"

Minutes passed with neither saying a word. He hated that deep down inside he felt he could never be enough for Micah. But what if this was the universe's way of pushing him to be more?

"So, wait. Go back. Tell me what happened after she sent you that text message. What did you say in response?"

"Well, I went over there. No matter what, I couldn't say anything to her through text message."

"Right. That is always a bad idea."

"She was crying and you could tell just how much she hadn't wanted me to know. She was stressing about it to the max."

"What did you tell her?"

"I told her I couldn't do it."

"You couldn't do what?"

"I couldn't be with her. I could not do this with her."

"Are you freaking kidding me?"

"No. What was I supposed to say?"

"I don't know. *Anything* but that."

"This sucks! I don't know what to do to make it better."

"You tell her the truth. You tell her you love her and that you are a freaking idiot and you can't live without her."

"You don't understand."

"You're right. I don't."

"I'll figure it out later. I don't want to think any more about it right now. Why are we wasting time talking about relationships like a bunch of girls when there is a perfectly good football game about to start?"

"Seriously, though. Don't be an idiot and let her get away."

"Okay. You're done. Football game is on." Josh turned up the volume and let the announcer's voice drown out his friend as well as his thoughts.

It didn't work, though. The game was on but Josh wasn't watching. How had everything spiraled out of control so quickly? Ten years. It had been ten years since Drew's death and the vow he had made. He had successfully kept it a secret for a decade, and now it all threatened to crumble.

Jamie gave advice so freely, but if he knew the truth he would understand.

"Here, have another beer. I can hear the wheels turning in your head." Jamie handed him a bottle of beer, but he waved it off.

"No. I don't need it."

The memories of that night had haunted him for such a long time. It had always kept a much-needed wall between him and Micah. He wasn't sure when, but she had climbed over it, demolishing the barrier.

"You ready to make me understand?"

"I don't know, man." Josh dragged the palm of his hand down his face. It was all too much. Maybe he should talk about it. Get it out in the open, so to speak. "She doesn't know the truth about Drew's death."

"What do you mean?"

"It was my fault."

The look on Jamie's face told him he didn't believe him. Josh knew what he was thinking. Drew had been alone when he died. No other cars to blame. No other passengers to distract him.

"I know what you're thinking. He was driving too fast and it was raining. But...see, Drew called me. He was on the phone with me when he died."

"Oh, man..." Jamie leaned forward on the couch and rested his elbows on his knees.

"We were arguing."

"About what?"

"Micah." Josh took a deep breath. "I've always been in love with her and Drew knew it. He was setting me straight, telling me how it was going to be."

Jamie remained still as Josh spoke. "It was because of me that he wasn't paying attention, that he was going so fast. I can still remember everything. The screeching, the shattering, the twisting. I didn't know where he was or what had happened. I was too afraid to hang up on him to call for help. So I kept talking to him."

"Oh, God. Josh, why didn't you tell us?"

"What was I supposed to say?" Josh leaned forward and put his head in his hands. "I sat there in my truck in the middle of the rain and listened to our best friend take his last breath."

He fought to shake the memories from his head. He didn't want to think about Drew's last words just now.

"Once I snapped out of it, I ran into the house and called 911. It took awhile to figure everything out, but eventually I found myself standing in front of the wreckage. The paramedics had already left. They had taken him away in a body bag. Nothing left to do. Bright red-and-blue lights flashed all around as the police officers investigated and tried to make sense of what happened."

Josh remembered standing there as a deluge of heavy raindrops soaked through his thick coat. It was then that he took on the massive weight of guilt. Putting it on his shoulders like a cloak. It was all his fault. It was there in that moment that Josh had vowed never to breathe a word of this to Micah. She would hate him forever if she knew the truth. He would keep his promise and watch over her. He would protect her and never cross over the boundaries of friendship. He would do it for Drew.

"You know what happened. Drew's car lost control. He was going way too fast when he took that turn on Elk Street. By that point there was no way he could have avoided that tree. The car didn't stand a chance with an immovable oak. Instead it just wrapped around it. The misshapen mass of metal that I saw bore no resemblance to a vehicle. No one could have survived something like that. If I hadn't done something that day to piss him off, Drew wouldn't have been upset. He wouldn't have called me while driving in the pouring rain. He wouldn't have been driving so recklessly. He wouldn't have taken that corner so fast. But because of me, he did."

"Josh, we both know that Drew was a reckless driver no matter what mood he was in. He was always talking on the phone. Always going too fast. He was careless. It wasn't your fault. You just were unfortunate enough to be the one he was talking to at the time. It could have been any one of us."

Josh heard him. Knew he was speaking the truth. If Micah had been the one on the phone with Drew, he wouldn't have placed the blame on her shoulders. But even if it could all be reasoned away, he still couldn't get past the guilt or the promise he'd made.

"Did he die quickly? Did he say anything?" Josh had never considered the fact that he was the only one aware of Drew's last moments. It had all been a mystery to his family and friends. He was selfish for keeping it secret all these years.

"It was pretty quick. It all happened so fast. It could have been mere seconds, but it felt like an eternity. Hearing him and not being able to do anything... He didn't say much. Each word was a struggle. But Micah's name was the last he said." He leaned back into the couch, emotionally depleted. "Jamie, I made a promise then and there that I would always protect her, and that included protecting her from me. Which, obviously, I've failed at."

"Josh, I can't say I would have handled it any differently, but still... Listen, we've been talking to Micah about letting go and moving on, and she's finally doing it. Now I think it's your turn. Drew would never have blamed you for what happened. It's time you let that go."

Talking had helped get it all out there so he could finally work through it. Jamie was right. He did need to let it go. For himself. For Micah.

He only wanted to do what was best for her. She deserved more than what he had to offer. Even days after the mistaken text message, the fact that she had said she had fallen in love with him still hadn't sunk in yet. How could this be? He wasn't deserving of someone like her. He didn't deserve to be loved like that.

He knew women found him attractive, wanted to date him, but they did not fall in love with him. He usually did something to screw it up long before they got to that point.

So when had it happened with Micah? Was it really possible that she had seen past his idiocy and in spite of his numerous flaws had really fallen in love with him? She knew him better than anyone, better than most of his family, and still she claimed to love him.

It blew his mind.

Should he tell her? Would she still love him after she knew the truth?

He felt it was only right that she know everything once and for all. If she could so bravely reveal her heart to him, the least he could do was tell her the truth.

While men fought over a football on the television screen and Jamie sat beside him feigning interest in the game, Josh grew closer and closer to a decision. He knew well Jamie was just biding his time until Josh came to the right conclusion.

"I should talk to her," Josh finally said.

"You should."

The more time that had passed, the closer he was to doing something about it. He needed some courage and clarity of mind.

Josh knew that if he broke her heart, he would never forgive himself. But he also knew that if he let this moment pass him by and watched as some other man came and stole her away, he would regret it for the rest of his days. He had nothing left to lose.

"This is crazy. I have never had a problem talking to a woman before. Why am I so worked up over her?"

"Because she's not just *any* girl. She's Micah."

He did not want to admit it out loud, but it scared him to death. Nothing had frightened him more in his entire life than the thought of facing Micah and telling her that he had lied. He could not imagine the amount of courage it would take to tell her that he was in love with her and had been since the moment he laid eyes on her.

He remembered the first day he met her. She'd been so vibrant, with her fiery hair flowing wildly in the wind. Her soft brown eyes turned a glowing shade of bronze when the sun hit her just right. She was carefree in her cotton, summery dress that seemed to dance in the breeze. He remembered the color, even—a jade green. He loved how it looked against her ivory skin and how bright it made her eyes look when you got close to her.

The jealousy he'd felt when he found out she belonged to another, to Drew, was like nothing he had ever experienced before in his life. The intensity of it had gutted him to the core.

But that was just it. She didn't belong to anyone. She didn't belong to Drew and she didn't belong to him, either. He had been trying to protect her, but instead had been controlling her. Regardless of how much she fought it, he kept treating her like a possession. She had a mind, a beautiful mind, of her own. She deserved to know all of the facts. She deserved to be able to make the decision for herself.

Ah! He felt like such a dumb ass. When it came to Micah, he just couldn't think straight. He needed to talk to her.

When he finally came to a decision, he stood up and walked out the door without another word to Jamie. He was sure he could figure out what was about to happen.

CHAPTER SEVENTEEN

JOSH FOUND HIMSELF standing in front of the door to Micah's apartment. He wasn't sure how long he had been standing there—at least several minutes—trying to gather up the nerve to knock.

His stomach churned. His hands felt tingly as the adrenaline pumped through his veins. In his line of work, he went head-to-head with serious fires and life-and-death situations, but this five-foot-six-inch fiery redhead had to be the scariest encounter he had ever faced.

Josh took in a deep, stabilizing breath before lifting his hand and knocking on the door. He heard footsteps. His heartbeat became so loud it drowned out the noise. The door opened; he held his breath. When he saw Sabina on the other side of the threshold, he let it out in a whoosh.

"Is Micah around?"

"*Is Micah around?* You've got some nerve showing up h—"

"Sabina, I don't really feel like getting into it with you right now. I just need to talk to her."

"Well, I am thinking you pretty much screwed up your chance to talk to her the other night."

"Come on, just let me in."

"I would, but she's not even here. She went out with Hanna." Then, as if she needed to throw salt in the wound, she said, "She went to meet some new guys. It is about time she met someone decent."

"Listen, I know you have never been fond of me and we have had our differences. And I will be the first to say that Micah deserves more than what I have to offer, but I do love her. I am a stupid idiot and I may have ruined everything, but I need to at least make it right."

"That is sweet and everything, but for real, she is not here. I think you've missed your shot, buddy." Sabina closed the door on him, leaving him staring at the fall wreath that hung on the door.

He took a step back and was met with the wall. Leaning against it, he slowly lowered himself to the floor. What was he doing? He should leave. He should pretend he had not let Jamie talk him into this ridiculous idea. Micah would never know. He could text Sabina and ask her to keep quiet—judging by her reaction to him, like a mama bear protecting her baby, he knew she would agree and keep it between them.

He brought his knees up, propped his elbows on them and dropped his head in his hands. He really should just leave, but he couldn't do it. He needed to see her the way he needed his next breath. Nothing would ever be the same if she was not a part of his life.

Hanna dropped Micah off after a night of failed attempts at meeting eligible men and maybe one too many cocktails. There were a few possibilities that she'd felt held some potential. But each guy she met would smile at her and flirt with her, but in the end they just came up short. One by one she knocked them down.

Not Josh.

Not Josh.

Nope.

Definitely not even close to being Josh.

The guys seemed to be interested in her, which she took as a good sign, but she hadn't been able to find any that she was interested in. Maybe in time she would. She was not giving up just yet. She would find someone.

In the meantime, it was going to be a lot of fun getting to know who she really was apart from all that she had been hiding behind.

Micah rounded the corner, climbed the last flight of steps to the third floor and noticed him sitting there in front of her door, as if he was waiting for her. She closed her eyes and opened them again, wondering if maybe she had just conjured up his image.

He looked up at her, his eyes filled with pain and regret. Her heart broke all over again seeing him sitting there. He stood and wiped his hands down the front of his jeans. He wore a navy hoodie, the one with his firefighter emblem on the chest. She always thought he looked invincible yet huggable when wearing that hoodie. But she couldn't hug him anymore. Not right now, at least. Or maybe any time soon.

"I needed to talk to you. I had to see you."

"What for?"

"I shouldn't have...I should have told you the truth." He ran his hand through his hair. She could see the evidence of stress and pain all over his face. "I...uh...I lied, Micah."

"What do you mean?

"Give me a moment. This is difficult for me."

Josh looked down at his feet, shoved his hands in his pockets, then pulled them out again. He seemed nervous. She had never seen him like this before. It was an unsettling sight. At the same time it warmed her heart and showed a side of him that was vulnerable in a way she did not know he could be.

She found herself fidgeting as well, playing with her keys and fumbling with the strap of her purse on her shoulder.

"I lied the other night. I was a being a coward. A coward and a liar. I would completely understand if you never wanted to talk to me again, but I just need to tell you the truth."

She said nothing, just nodded her head for him to continue. She was all ears.

"I was afraid." He still looked down at his feet, avoiding eye contact. "I was afraid that if I told you the truth that I would lose you."

"Lose me? You could never lose me, unless you push me away." Then again, he had lost her in a way, even if it was temporary.

His hands went back in his pockets.

This whole scene was beginning to make her nervous, too. Especially with how nervous he was acting right now. "What truth are you talking about?"

He lifted his head, the full force of his gray eyes enveloping her under his spell. It was as if he summoned all his courage and took a deep breath. His eyes dropped to her lips, then back up to her eyes.

"Micah..." It came out as a breath, barely a whisper. Her name on his lips said more to her than anything else. The one word was filled with so much emotion and reverence, and so many unknowns.

"Drew called me right before the accident. We were arguing when he lost control."

She gasped, her hand covering her open mouth. "Oh, Josh."

He didn't look up. She wanted so badly to comfort him, but stopped herself. He needed to say this. He needed to get it out. She knew all too well the powerful grip that grief could have on you. He had to release it.

"He was angry with me. Over you. I shouldn't have… I wish I had… I'm sorry, Mike."

She could see it in his eyes. He had carried the weight of guilt, blaming himself for the accident. She went to him then, wrapped her arms around his waist, leaned her head on his chest. "Why are you apologizing? It was an accident, Josh. It wasn't your fault."

She felt the tension slowly ease from his shoulders. He pulled back from her enough to look into her eyes. "Your name was the last thing he said. I promised him I would take care of you. Maybe I took that job a little too seriously. I don't know."

He pulled away completely, walked to the end of the hallway then back. "I've tried. You have to believe me. I've tried so hard to keep my promise to him. I built a wall around you to keep you safe, even from me, but you scaled it. I just wanted to protect you. And I realized it was never about the promise. It was you. It's always been you. You grabbed hold of my heart and I can't let you go. Something keeps pulling me back to you. You have a hold on me that I can't seem to break—that I don't want to break."

"What are you saying?"

"Micah—" his eyes dropped to her lips again "—I need you to kiss me." Josh stepped closer, but not close enough. "I need to feel your lips against mine. I need to taste you one more time. I can't go another moment without kissing you again."

Frozen, unable to move, she stood there as he inched

closer to her still. His head dipped low, coming in close to hers without touching, his lips only a breath away from her own. She felt the warm rush of air, the sweet smell of his breath as he hovered over her mouth.

Ever the gentleman when it came to her, she knew he wouldn't kiss her without her approval. If this kiss was going to happen, she had to be the one to make that final step. She only needed to lean forward; he was less than an inch away. But once that happened, it meant there was no going back to the way things were.

She didn't *ever* want to go back to that.

Without a second thought, she closed the gap and pressed her lips home. She poured every ounce of emotion she had into the kiss, holding nothing back. If they were going to do this, really do this, then he needed to know how she truly felt. His lips molded to hers as if they were made to be together.

He slowly began to pull back. She did not want it to end, but knew the kiss was growing in intensity. Maybe the hallway outside her front door was not the best place for this to happen. His hands came around to gently grasp her forearms, pulling her hands away from his chest. His fingers slid down her arms until he had her hands within his at their sides. He placed several small kisses to her lips, as if needing to end the kiss but not being able to find the strength to do it.

"Micah." He said her name against her lips. That had to be the sexiest thing she had ever experienced. Granted, her sexy experiences were limited.

"Hmm." It was the only response she could manage at this moment.

"I love you."

Her eyes snapped open. "You do?"

"Yes." He still had not completely pulled away. He took their intertwined hands and wrapped his arms around her, forcing her hands back as well. "Sorry I was such an idiot and was too afraid to say it before. I was a coward."

"*Coward* is that last word I would ever use to describe you." She pulled back to see his face in full while he talked, to be able to read his eyes. "What were you so scared of?"

"Many things. I was scared that you would blame me for Drew's death..."

"Never."

"The thought of losing you scared me the most, but stupidly, I almost lost you, anyway. I knew when you kissed me the night of the snowstorm that I was in deep trouble. That there was no way I was getting out of this unscathed. That was frightening."

"You mean the morning *after* the snowstorm. We kissed in the snow, not the night before."

"We kissed the night before and the next morning. You seriously can't remember?" A laugh exploded from deep within him.

Her hand went to her mouth in shock. Her mind raced to piece together the memories of that night. Heat crept up the back of her neck. "I thought I was dreaming!"

"I wondered. When you were completely oblivious to the fact you tried to jump my bones the night before, I wondered if maybe you had experienced a little bit of sleepwalking. Oh, you tested my limits that night!"

She let her forehead fall to his chest, not wanting to look him in the eyes. She couldn't help the smile that formed on her face, nor could she deny that she had indeed tried to jump his bones that night.

But come on, she'd thought she had been within the safety and anonymity of a dream!

He kissed the top of her head as he reined in his laughter and continued. "You threw me for a loop that night, and I was terrified. I was scared of the emotions I was feeling. I have never felt anything like that before."

She felt giddy, like a little schoolgirl with her first crush, only better. "You haven't?"

"No. This is all new to me. Maybe that's why it took me so long to figure it out."

"Show me how you feel again." She grabbed the back of his neck and brought his face down to meet her own.

He didn't hesitate for a moment, showing her exactly how he felt about her with a kiss that, if she'd been wearing socks, would have knocked them clean off. He kissed her as though he couldn't get enough of her, and she felt the same thing. She never wanted this to end.

They stood there in the hallway, completely unaware of their surroundings. She placed her hand on the side of his face, needing the confirmation that he was real and not another dream playing tricks on her.

"I love you, Micah, and I don't ever want to let you go. You're the first woman I've ever said that to, you know. I want you to be the first woman I bring home to meet my family, too."

She actually felt herself blushing. She hadn't seen them in years, but she still knew his family well. "I've already met your family, you goof."

"I know, but still. I want them to see you as the woman I love, not just the girl I was friends with. Still sounds strange to my own ears, but I don't think I could grow tired of telling you. I love you, Micah."

"I love you, too, Josh." She threw her arms around his neck and kissed him again.

Who would have guessed this would ever come about? She'd never thought the day would come that she would be in the middle of the hallway in her apartment building, kissing Josh Taylor with abandon. *My, my,* how life had a way of taking you by surprise. And all it took was letting go of the past and allowing herself to embrace the here and now.

She really had missed out on a lot during that time, but she was not going to let it get her down. No, she was only going to focus on making the most of today. And at the moment, that involved relishing the divine rush caused by the touch of Josh's hands. His skillful lips felt like heaven and his arms held her tight, as if they never wanted to let her go.

His hands came up to frame her face. And as he kissed her softly this time, she felt his fingertips graze her neck and slip beneath the collar of her jacket. He pushed it off her shoulders as he broke away from her lips and kissed a path down the sensitive part of her neck. He turned her in his arms so that she was facing away from him but still nestled within his grasp. His lips continued their divine assault down the delicate slope of her shoulders. She let her head fall back against him as he pushed the strap of her dress aside.

"I just have one more question."

"Hmm…"

He placed a kiss over the tiny heart tattoo that graced her left shoulder.

"Is this…?"

"Yes." She knew what he wanted to know before he even voiced it. "I went to get it done and as I sat there and waited for my turn, I realized what I really wanted was *your* heart. And this is how you always sign your text messages to me."

She turned in his arms, needing to see the face she loved so dearly. "When did you see it?"

"I noticed it during the snowstorm." He kissed her again, then spoke the words against the side of her mouth. "I wanted it to be me."

* * * * *

Mills & Boon® Hardback
July 2014

ROMANCE

Christakis's Rebellious Wife	Lynne Graham
At No Man's Command	Melanie Milburne
Carrying the Sheikh's Heir	Lynn Raye Harris
Bound by the Italian's Contract	Janette Kenny
Dante's Unexpected Legacy	Catherine George
A Deal with Demakis	Tara Pammi
The Ultimate Playboy	Maya Blake
Socialite's Gamble	Michelle Conder
Her Hottest Summer Yet	Ally Blake
Who's Afraid of the Big Bad Boss?	Nina Harrington
If Only...	Tanya Wright
Only the Brave Try Ballet	Stefanie London
Her Irresistible Protector	Michelle Douglas
The Maverick Millionaire	Alison Roberts
The Return of the Rebel	Jennifer Faye
The Tycoon and the Wedding Planner	Kandy Shepherd
The Accidental Daddy	Meredith Webber
Pregnant with the Soldier's Son	Amy Ruttan

MEDICAL

200 Harley Street: The Shameless Maverick	Louisa George
200 Harley Street: The Tortured Hero	Amy Andrews
A Home for the Hot-Shot Doc	Dianne Drake
A Doctor's Confession	Dianne Drake

Mills & Boon® Large Print

July 2014

ROMANCE

HISTORICAL

MEDICAL

Mills & Boon® Hardback
August 2014

ROMANCE

Zarif's Convenient Queen	Lynne Graham
Uncovering Her Nine Month Secret	Jennie Lucas
His Forbidden Diamond	Susan Stephens
Undone by the Sultan's Touch	Caitlin Crews
The Argentinian's Demand	Cathy Williams
Taming the Notorious Sicilian	Michelle Smart
The Ultimate Seduction	Dani Collins
Billionaire's Secret	Chantelle Shaw
The Heat of the Night	Amy Andrews
The Morning After the Night Before	Nikki Logan
Here Comes the Bridesmaid	Avril Tremayne
How to Bag a Billionaire	Nina Milne
The Rebel and the Heiress	Michelle Douglas
Not Just a Convenient Marriage	Lucy Gordon
A Groom Worth Waiting For	Sophie Pembroke
Crown Prince, Pregnant Bride	Kate Hardy
Daring to Date Her Boss	Joanna Neil
A Doctor to Heal Her Heart	Annie Claydon

MEDICAL

Tempted by Her Boss	Scarlet Wilson
His Girl From Nowhere	Tina Beckett
Falling For Dr Dimitriou	Anne Fraser
Return of Dr Irresistible	Amalie Berlin

Mills & Boon® Large Print

August 2014

ROMANCE

HISTORICAL

MEDICAL

Discover more romance at

www.millsandboon.co.uk

- ❤ WIN great prizes in our exclusive competitions
- ❤ BUY new titles before they hit the shops
- ❤ BROWSE new books and REVIEW your favourites
- ❤ SAVE on new books with the Mills & Boon® Bookclub™
- ❤ DISCOVER new authors

PLUS, to chat about your favourite reads, get the latest news and find special offers:

- Find us on facebook.com/millsandboon
- Follow us on twitter.com/millsandboonuk
- ❤ Sign up to our newsletter at millsandboon.co.uk